DEDICATION:

TO MY LATE HUSBAND,
ROBERT BUCK

Introduction

"When we meet real tragedy in life, we can react in two ways –
either by losing hope and falling into self-destructive habits,
or by using the challenge to find our inner strength."

- The Dalai Lama

When I was a little girl growing up in the rural area of China, I had no idea what my life purpose would be. Even as an adult, I still hadn't figured out how I should live my life. I was always living in survival mode.

Finally, I started my normal life after I married a wonderful man who loved me beyond all measure. But ten years later, he got sick and left me as a young widow. My first startling moment, a glimpse at the work that would need to be done to survive once again, came through a simple cup of coffee. I was traveling alone, soon after the death of my husband, when I went to take a sip of coffee and spilled all over myself. I had not tightened the lid to the cup. It had not occurred to me. My beloved husband did everything, even tighten lids.

My late husband had been my source of care, happiness, love, and confidence. After I lost him, I slowly realized that I needed to find all these qualities within myself. This was the beginning of my trajectory from widow to an empowered human being. I began to transform my life from surviving to thriving. During that time, I found comfort in writing to capture my thoughts and track my progress. It was powerful and led to rapid healing and growth. I started blogging through the journey of *Life After Loss* and *Being the Best of Me*. You may be a reader who has followed me on my website *colorandgrace.com*. Those blog posts have now been reinvented, organized, and expanded into this book, *Finding Grace*. This is the first in a series of books I hope to create to inspire, lead, and help people to heal as they move through grief or loss of any kind.

I've designed *Finding Grace* as a fast read with direct life lessons so that anyone can read it and step away as needed until they are more prepared to continue the journey. I'm humbly proud of what's been created, especially considering that English is a second language for me. I hope you will enjoy *Finding Grace* and are inspired to create your best possible life, regardless of what you already have or don't have. This book is not only for people of humble beginnings and/or loss but for the successful individual who wishes to continue on that trajectory, as well as those seeking deeper purpose.

Please follow me online where you will find information on our empowerment and writing workshops, speaking engagements, outreach opportunities, and professional friendship.

www.colorandgrace.com

Thank you for reading about how I found *Grace*, in every way...and a name I providentially chose for myself when I came to the United States.

"Grief is in two parts. The first is loss. The second is the remaking of life."

— Anne Roiphe, Writer

PART ONE

Grace's Story

(1974–2007)

From Humble Beginnings, A New Story Is Born

"It matters not what someone is born, but what they grow to be."

-J.K. Rowling

I grew up in northeast China. My hometown is about midway between the borders of what was once the USSR and North Korea. We had the terrible combination of Russian winters and Democratic People's Republic of Korea (DPRK, also known as North Korea) fashion! This part of China is peppered with blue collar factory cities and rural villages. I lived in both as a child.

My late husband grew up in a typical upper-middle class American family—nice house with a pool, stay-at-home mom, four kids, two dogs, family vacations, and a color TV. Pretty fortunate. My childhood was filled with hunger, tears, and frostbite! We barely held on to a small house with a straw roof and dirt floor. We had no running water nor an indoor toilet. I had never had a toy, a TV, nor a bike. I didn't see a private car until I was eleven years old when we moved to a small city. I loved sitting on the side of the road just watching cars driving by. It was all very fascinating!

Most Asian cultures have traditionally valued sons above daughters, and my family was no different. I was never coddled as a young girl and often was mistaken for a boy as I would wear my hair short and dress in my older brother's hand-me-down clothes. It's not surprising that no one thought of me as beautiful, including myself! It really wasn't until I became an adult and moved away to live in the much more modern and glamorous city of Shanghai that I even began to see myself as anything other than plain looking at best.

Below is a poem that my dear, late husband wrote for me based on my life story from the year I was born in 1974, until the year I moved to America to marry him in 2007.

Grace's Life Story

I was born in China, child number two.
My brother was first, more popular too.
The culture has said that boys are the choice.
Girls like me don't get a big voice.
Because girls are below and boys are above,
I really don't feel I got my mom's love.

When I was young, I was poorer than poor
Straw was our roof and dirt for our floor.
The kitchen was special; it held our one pot.
But we had little food more often than not.
Money was tight so we couldn't buy rice.
My brother and I stole soybeans from mice.
My mom and my dad worked every day.
No time for weekends. No time for play.
Farming and factories, iron, and steel.
That was the way we paid for our meal.
Never heard of vacation. Hard work's all we knew.

That's what I learned. I still think it's true.

I played with my friends, but that was hard too.
We moved to a house so often; every neighbor was new.
Another new month, another new house,
Another new school, but same worn blouse.

Times were quite hard when I was a kid.
I'll never forget the way that we lived.
We didn't know birthdays or parties like here.
Our one celebration was Chinese New Year.
The only sure time I knew there'd be food,
Some small lucky money and new clothing, too.

The rest of the year was day after day
Of too much to do, for too little pay.
I hated the mud. I hated the dirt.
I hated the way that my feelings would hurt.

When I think of my childhood, I remember my fears.
And the terrible words that came to my ears.
"You're ugly, you're stupid, shut up, you can't sing.
Don't waste time pretending you'll be anything."
So, I knew sometime later, in several more years,
I'd leave this behind. This place of my tears.

It started with high school; I lived in a dorm.
And being away from home was my norm.
But the tears didn't stop; I often was sad.
And to make matters worse I now lost my dad.
But I got through high school, university too.
I now was a teacher with a job to do.
But I still didn't feel my life was my own.
I had to go further. I had to leave home.

I had a big dream; Shanghai was its name.
So, I packed my one bag and got on a train.
I showed up alone; no place to stay.
No one to talk to, and no way to pay.

It was far from easy, but I first found a bed
And then got a job to get myself fed.
I was determined to be a success,
At least not to fail, so no time to rest.
I wouldn't go home until I could prove
My decision was good; I'd been right to move.

The years came and went but finally I knew.
Now I could visit, and this time I flew.
I went back to Shanghai and made some new friends.
You might be thinking the story now ends.
But over in China, the sun also rises

On days filled with hope and sometimes surprises.
I'd sort of accepted it might stay just me
When I went out to eat with two friends, just us three.
We sat at a table and ordered some food.
Then three men sat beside us; I thought it was rude.
One thing quite different about the big city.
It's the first place I heard I might just be pretty.
It seemed that one of these men thought so too.
But he was American so what could I do?

It started quite slowly but before we knew.
I thought I'd stay one. But now we were two.
I'd never left China, for even a day.
Now home's in America, and that's where I'll stay.
So many things have changed in my life.

I learned how to drive and learned how to wife.
I'm still learning English, more all the time.
Now I speak it in dreams, so I think I'll be fine.

I guess those hard times I went through when young
Have made me the woman that I have become.
You can't have your now without the before.
You won't see what's rich without knowing poor.
I've come so far from that place that I hate.
I still can't believe life can be so great!

PART TWO

Living with Cancer

(2016–2017)

Keeping It Normal and Enjoying Every Moment We Can

"Since I've had cancer, I've realized that every day is a bonus."

- Geoffrey Boycott

October 28, 2016

It has been eight months since my man was diagnosed with his second bout with cancer. One night, while my husband and I were lying in bed, just before we said good night, my husband suddenly said, "I wish I could be normal again, someday."

I instantly cried. Tears were in my ears and my hair, and I just could not help it. "I am so sorry!" was all I could say.

"You didn't do anything wrong," my man answered.

"But I wish I could do something to save you." I couldn't help choking up again.

We all knew he may not have a *someday.* His doctor told us that Bob might have less than a year left. The cancer was super rare and aggressive. He was a fighter; however, the chemo and radiation had beaten him down very hard, even though he rarely said anything. One morning, he had a very hard time trying to button his shirt because his fingers were not working as they should. He drove over a curb that afternoon and in the evening, he knocked his water glass over onto some important files. It wasn't a good day for him.

There were a few friends who knew what we were going through. I tried to protect my family's privacy, so I never mentioned it in public. But then, one morning, I got a message from a friend asking me if I knew anything about the husband of one of my blogger friends. I read her post and I was shocked. They were going through a tough time very similar to ours. I cried the whole way to work that morning.

That day I wrote a special blog post––not for myself, but for my friend, and for those people out there whose name or story I may not know. I decided to announce my husband's cancer to the public. I wanted my friend, and anybody who was facing similar situations, to know that we are all in this together.

If God or Buddha, or whoever the higher power is, has decided to put an expiration date on the relationships we have with our loved ones, then we just make the best out of every day we have left.

My husband and I had both told our family and friends many times that we don't need a pity party. "Let's celebrate every day and every minute we are together. Let's go out while we can walk and enjoy the food while we can eat!"

Is the Glass Half-Full, or Half-Empty?

"Positive thinking is more than just a tagline.
It changes the way we behave.
And I firmly believe that when I am positive, it not only makes me
better, but it also makes those around me better."

-Harvey Mackay

November 11, 2016

I was holding parent/teacher conferences for my students. I had always put my phone on silent while I was at work. But since my husband was first diagnosed with skin cancer, in September 2015, I had the habit of checking my phone more often.

My morning was fully booked. I mean booked so tightly there wasn't even room for any bathroom breaks. However, while I was waiting on a late parent, I turned on my phone. There were two long text messages from my man. He'd had another episode where he almost passed out; this time he was at work. It had happened several times before. After resisting two types of chemo and radiation, the tumors on his neck and in his chest were growing back again. The one on his neck was pushing against his vein and caused him to get lightheaded and dizzy, especially if he turned his head a certain way. He had even passed out a couple of times.

This is the first time it happened while he was not with me. Bob said he was able to walk outside of the meeting room at work, but he had to sit on the floor. There was nobody there, and that scared me. What if he had lost consciousness and there was nobody to help him? What about when he was driving?

What do you think happened next? Of course, he drove home! We only lived a few miles from his office, but, still, he drove! His boss asked him if he wanted to have someone drive him, and a co-worker asked the same thing while he was walking out to his car. But you know men, and my man especially: "No, I'll be fine," he responded. Then he got in his car and drove off. I couldn't let my imagination go too far. He did make it home without any problem and laid down for a while. That took the pressure off the tumor and he felt much better. Yet, it still frightened me.

Saturday, we decided to have dim sum for brunch. While we were at the restaurant, he felt like he was going to pass out again. Luckily it was not a full attack. Sunday, it happened again. We were home this time, and he was able to walk to the bed where he laid down for an hour and again felt much better.

We were worried – at least, I was. Bob just became annoyed more than anything. Yet, we still enjoyed our life together. The next week on Saturday, after brunch, we went to a park nearby, the colorful leaves were so breathtaking. We even tried a new restaurant that evening, and he found his favorite short rib dish. All of this was to make the upcoming procedures more bearable.

As long as there was something we could do, we stayed positive. That's how we dealt with this problem; by focusing on what we could do instead of what we couldn't.

Are you looking at the glass half full or half empty?
We knew that as long as we could hold hands, look into each other's eyes, smile and laugh together, our glass would always be overflowing.

Live Each Day as If It Were Your Last

"It's only when we truly know and understand that we have a limited time on earth - and that we have no way of knowing when our time is up, we will then begin to live each day to the fullest, as if it was the only one we had."

- Elisabeth Kubler-Ross

November 25, 2016

My husband Bob and I have had a very difficult year. After having melanoma removed in the fall of 2015, we thought we were done with cancer, but it seemed that cancer wasn't done with us.

In February, his doctor found that he had lymphoma, and our whole year changed in that moment. The rest of the spring and my whole summer break from school was spent in waiting rooms, chemo infusion rooms, ERs, ICUs, and hospital rooms. There were CT scans, PET/CT scans, MRIs, X-rays, and so many blood draws my man often thought he was being mistaken for a pincushion!

We made it through the summer, and I was actually happy when school started again to give me a change of scenery. In early September, we had our open house at school with all the parents. It was a very successful night. When I got home at that evening, my man was waiting for me. We chatted more about my exciting night, and then I asked him about his doctor's appointment earlier that day. It sounded normal at first, but suddenly he said, "My doctor told me I may only have half a year left."

It took me several days to digest this news. I am not a cry baby at all, but this had me tearing up for a few days. I just held him and told him over and over, "I don't want you to die!" I know it's a silly thing to say, but that's all that would come out - along with my tears and mascara, which by now were all over his shirt.

In October, we went to see his doctor again. After two different types of chemo and one radiation proved to be ineffective, his doctor said he may only have three months left at this point. This particular cancer was super rare, and the doctor really just didn't know what exactly to do with it. Of course, that didn't make us feel any better; I just couldn't wrap my mind around this news. For the next several days, the tears continued to come back over and over. And there went some more of my husband's shirts. I just couldn't imagine my man might not being able to see Christmas.

The tumor came back very quickly again. It pushed against the vein on his neck and made his blood pressure either dangerously low or dangerously high. One day, just before we went to see his doctor again to start the third type of chemo, Bob yelled, "New record!" His blood pressure was 222 over 136. After we told his doctor about the blood pressure reading, the doctor said he was worried that my husband may have a stroke at any time. If that happened, they would have to stop all the treatments.

I asked the doctor what I could do to save him if it happened. He paused and said, "Give him a hug and kiss." Just when I thought I was finally drying out, here came my tears again. There were too many people in the room this time, so I used a box of tissues and left Bob's shirt alone.

The time with my man had been shortened again and again; but the love between us had never been greater. He was the toughest guy, and he was still trying to take care of me every day. We were both so happy we had found each other and, even with the trouble, we continued having so many good times together.

Sometimes it was mixed with tears and added another shirt in the hamper, but there was always laughter in our house. The saying, "Live each day as if it was your last" became our mantra.

We were living it every day. It was not because we were brave or strong. We chose to live to the fullest every day while we could still breathe. Life is too short, and none of us have time for regrets!

How Am I Holding Up in the Darkest Moments in My Life?

"You do what you can for as long as you can, and when you finally can't, you do the next best thing. You back up but you don't give up."

- Chuck Yeager

January 16, 2017

A lot of people have said they couldn't believe what I had gone through in my life based on how I look, speak, and act now. I have tried very, very hard to make things as normal as I could.

So how did I hold up in the darkest time of my life? I focused on my purpose. At that moment in my life, my purpose was giving my husband the best care I could. I made sure he was comfortable, warm and clean, all while protecting his dignity.

I have been the most spoiled woman on Earth. Before my husband became sick, I never filled my own gas tank. He gave me the best care a man could give a woman, so I was very grateful that I had the chance to take care of him.

He was the person who allowed me to experience unconditional love--not even my parents did that. He always said he was the luckiest man because he had me as his wife. I told him that I was the luckiest woman to have him as my husband. He gave me a family, which I never had before. I am loved, cared for, and respected.

I am still trying to put on makeup and to dress comfortably, because I don't want him to feel I am giving up on myself or on us. It is not the end of the world because we are still together, holding hands and smiling at each other.

Preparing for the End of Life

"People living deeply have no fear of death."

- Anais Nin

January 18, 2017

Few of us are comfortable talking about death, whether it is our own or a loved one's. It is a scary, even taboo, subject for many. Luckily, my husband and I were comfortable talking about it.

Actually, Bob and I could talk about anything, we didn't have any secrets from each other. We were soulmates. I know it sounds corny. I was very surprised to realize many years ago that my soulmate did not look like I'd imagined. First, he was not Chinese, didn't even speak Chinese––well, not much. He could say, "beer," in Chinese. He was not of my generation, and he was bald and overweight.

But soulmates are all about the souls, right? Nobody said two people have to match perfectly on the outside when you look at them. Except maybe in movies. My friend called us, "The Beauty and the Beast." You can guess which one of us was which! Yet, we didn't care what others had to say. Food tasted better when we were eating together. We had so much to talk about, even after being married many years. He was the one who was usually the smarty pants and made me laugh, but once in a while, I was able to throw out a joke and make him laugh very hard, too.

We called ourselves weirdos because we were just happy together and silly together no matter what. When he lost almost eighty pounds due to his cancer, we joked about how different the view was because he could see his toes.

During that time, I cried a lot. The doctors had given us the final countdown. First, they said maybe a year or two. Then maybe less than a year; then less than half a year, then three months, and then, maybe less than eight weeks. I've often cried so hard I almost choked. Bob would say something very funny and make me laugh again.

We talked a lot about the end of life. He said he had no regrets at all. We have traveled around the world, tasted many yummy and strange foods, and created countless joyful moments. Our relationship and love were so rare and pure that we were lucky to have found each other in this lifetime. Yet, I worried how I would react when the time came, and Bob was no longer with me.

I had lost my dad to cancer when I was in high school. I totally shut down for three days without saying a single word or crying; I was shocked and angry. I was like a zombie, and my friends were so worried.

This was a lot harder than losing my dad. My man was not just my husband; he was also my best friend and a father figure. It would be like losing three people at the same time.

It didn't matter how much we prepared, when it happened, I knew my heart and world would be shattered.

PART THREE
Life After Loss

(2017–2018)

Announcement

"The song is ended, but the melody lingers on…"

- Irving Berlin

January 26, 2017 - Detroit (Day 1)

I know some of you have already heard the news about my husband, Robert Buck's, passing. I wanted to let everyone know that he was surrounded by family and was very peaceful in the final hours.

He was the best husband and my best friend. For the last ten years, I was the most spoiled wife on Earth. He took the best care of me and our family. I was very grateful that I had the chance to stay with him and take care of him. All of those precious moments will give me strength to carry on.

Thank you, everybody, for the great support you have given to us this last year. I was very proud to see Bob has touched so many people's lives.

If you had the chance to meet him, you know he was such a fun person to be around and how much he loved bringing fun and laughter to others. So instead of a sad funeral, he has asked for a big, happy party to celebrate his life. Adult beverages are a must-have. He wanted everybody to share the great moments and a memory you had with him or us. We will have this party in the spring.

We would love to hear any great memories you had with him, as I have found those stories bring me so much comfort at this difficult time. So, please, don't hesitate to reach out to me. If you prefer, you can pay tribute by donating to the Double Hit Lymphoma Foundation. Help them find a cure to save more people who have been diagnosed with the same rare type of cancer as Bob.

Please see the below obituary written by my stepdaughter, Ashley Buck. And please, say a toast for him next time you have a drink.

Obituary for Robert Buck

There once was a man named Bob Buck,
For the most part, he had lots of luck!
He loved to travel the world, both far and near,
He loved to eat food, and drink lots of beer.
In his fifty-nine years, he had a great life,
Two kids, two grandkids, an amazing wife!
He did auto design; his ideas were divine.
Worked at Magna thirty years. He put in his time.
Then the cancer came in, he said, "I'll be fine."
He gave a great fight but lost it in time.
He liked to tell jokes, to see everyone's laughter.
He loved having fun; he was such a fighter!
He loved his grand-dog,
His dirty straw hats,
Countless nieces and nephews,
Cannonballs in the pool,
And don't forget the frequent Bar-B-Qs!

The youngest of four, he also leaves his brother, his sisters,
His ninety-four-year-old father and so many others.
But don't be sad; this isn't the end,

The party continues for his family and friends.

Stay positive and laugh, and our hearts will eventually mend.
We'll never forget the joy he did bring,

We'll laugh and tell stories, sometime in the spring.
There won't be a service but a celebration of life.
He told us, "Have a big party instead, do not be sad."
So that's what we'll do, for our awesome dad.

Conquering Grief and Finding Hope

"What we once enjoyed and deeply loved we can never lose,
for all that we love deeply becomes part of us."
- Helen Keller

I had intentionally avoided talking about my family in order to protect them from the public eye. But now I think it is time to let more people know about my husband and how amazing he was––not only through my eyes, but through his children's as well.

Below is the post my stepson, Bobby, wrote:

> *"As many of you may or may not realize I never really post. I like to make them count, I guess.*
>
> *Today, my dad passed away. He had just put up a year-long fight with Double-Hit Lymphoma. From what I've seen, it's one of, if not the most aggressive and difficult lymphatic cancers we know of.*
>
> *While it is one of the saddest days of my life, and we exchanged no words today, he has caused every one of the many laughs I've had today. He was a strong, smart, and funny guy. He had a joke, appropriate or otherwise, for everything. He always had an answer too. But he would*

want us to celebrate his life, not be sad at his passing. So, from here on out I'll do my best to only shed tears from laughing at his jokes and memories. Next time any of you have a drink or a barbeque, tell a joke in his honor and raise a small toast.

Dad, I'll think back fondly on our time together. My nearly thirty years was far too short to lose you, but I've had so many good memories that you will never truly be gone. You'll be with me for every episode of Star Trek, James Bond movie, and read through of Lord of the Rings, you're in every Ford Focus, Dodge Challenger, and every other car you helped design. I am who I am because of you and I wouldn't have it any other way.

I miss you and love you, Dad. See you around, Baldy."

And here is the post from my stepdaughter, Ashley:

"For those of you who don't know, my dad has been fighting a very rare, aggressive form of lymphoma for the past year. It is something he wanted to keep private, so I have respected his wishes by keeping it off of Facebook. The prognosis was not good. Most people do not make it beyond six months after diagnosis. He made it nearly one year.

My dad was/is one of the best, most positive, funny people I know. Rather than sit back and take it, he put up a very impressive fight. Over ten types of chemo and so many rounds I lost track. Plus, multiple rounds of radiation and countless hospital stays. Most people would have given up, but every time it was suggested, he was positive that this was not how it would end. Each treatment stopped working in time, but rather than giving up, he asked what was next. Through everything, he never lost his positivity, humor, sarcasm, wit, and enthusiasm to live.

He was determined to beat it and gave it hell. We have tried to make light of it. When he had to get a walker, I blinged it out for him immediately, including flashing lights and a bell. If you can't laugh, you have nothing. Cancer can take a lot of things from the people it touches, and I'm glad his wit, humor, and positive outlook were with him till the end.

Today, I lost my dad just before 2:00 p.m. It feels surreal and wrong. I'm pretty sure I'm still in shock. There's no way this can be happening, but I know deep down it is. Like he's going to text me and be like, "Just kidding." It's something we knew was a real possibility, but never seemed real. I'm happy with how much time I've spent with him over the past year and have no regrets. I'm proud of how we all handled it together. We will get through it. It will suck, but I promised him we'd all be fine and that is one promise I will keep. I love you, Dad, and always will. I'm sorry I didn't say it more, even though I know you knew so without me saying it. I hope wherever you are, you're giving them hell.

It has been super difficult, but my family and I are doing pretty well as you can see here. We still eat, drink, and play card games. Just like the obituary said, we are honoring him by picking ourselves up and enjoying our lives again, even though now it is without him. We can't see him anymore, but he is right here in our hearts and will continue to live through us."

Remembering My Man with Honor and in Gratitude

"If the people we love are stolen from us,
the way to have them live on is to never stop loving them."

- James O'Barr

February 20, 2017 (Day 26)

It has been almost one month since my man passed away. I was in one of those holes I had found myself in more often recently. I thought I was brave enough to handle the loss of Bob. I also thought we prepared enough so that I would be okay. I wasn't. I was so used to sharing every little detail of my life with him. I found myself talking to his ashes or just the air more and more often.

I wanted to tell him how grateful I was because of the love I received from my family, friends, students, co-workers, and all the other nice people in my life. I also wanted to tell him that I didn't use GPS to go to our favorite restaurant. I know he would have been proud of me.

But it was just me talking, and there was no response at all. Those monologues usually quickly turned into crying spells; sometimes long, sometimes short. I didn't know I had that many tears in me. Soon the sadness became anger. These spells usually ended with trying to remember what he used to say when I was crying. He always knew what to say or to do to make me feel better. I knew I needed to pick myself up and move forward, even if it was just a little; even if it felt like I was going backwards.

I sometimes felt like he had just gone on a business trip, and he would be back home someday. But slowly, I realized deep down, he was gone forever. And those realizations hurt so much!

Somehow, I began to heal.

I survived Valentine's Day. I didn't cry. I wasn't even moody. Then, one day I suddenly noticed when I looked at his photo, I didn't cry. I smiled. A few evenings ago, I came to a conclusion: His physical body was gone, but his love was still with me.

His life would continue through my eyes, my heart, and my life. With that thought, I had a giant smile on my face. A door toward happiness suddenly opened for me. This was not just my life now; it was still ours. We were still together, just in a different way!

Slowly, I began doing things that he once did for us. When I went out to see some friends, I ordered Moscato wine. I even asked where I could buy it for later. This was something Bob would usually do. It felt so good to try new things that he would enjoy. I even tried to be a smarty pants during my work meetings because that was what he used to do. Everybody remembered his quick wit.

Recently, I went out with a friend, and she told me she was worried that the whole evening would have been filled with tears. I was totally fine because I could see my man's smiling face in my head all the time.

When you really love someone, you want to honor that person with what they want. He wanted me, and my family, to continue to enjoy our lives, and that is what we are doing.

Carrying on My Husband's Legacy

> *"Legacy is not leaving something for people.*
> *It's leaving something in people."*
> - Peter Strople

March 6, 2017 (Day 40)

My husband was just a simple guy who enjoyed his life very much. He didn't have any big ambitions or dreams. He just wanted to make every day a happy day.

He loved food very much; not just eating. He *loved* cooking too, especially BBQ in our backyard. He literally barbecued all year round, even in the winter. He was a charcoal guy. He had the whole system down, from the charcoal starter to the beer BBQ method. He even convinced a few of his friends and co-workers to switch to charcoal.

Bob loved to make people laugh. I am pretty sure that when he was young, he was a class clown. People show humor in many ways - some are cruel, some are stupid, and some have a dry humor. His was always very smart and harmless. He could easily break any serious or tense situation with his humor. Many of his co-workers have told me that they really miss his quick wit.

Overall, my man was the guy with a general love for life. This was the biggest legacy he left me. I tended to worry a lot, but after the many years we were together, I started to see a difference in my own beliefs and behavior. Now I know it doesn't matter what happens, it's important to always eat well and sleep well, because most likely we will still have tomorrow to start over again. There is really nothing that can be *that* big of a deal most of the time.

One month after my man passed away, I noticed I was doing pretty well taking care of myself. I cut my morning fruit the night before and cooked breakfast for myself every day. I never skipped any meals, because I could hear his voice in my head yelling at me. I tried to let my humor out more; I still needed a *lot* of practice. I may never be a smarty pants like him, but at least I have loosened up quite bit. It has not been very easy for an uptight Asian woman.

I learned that it was up to me to live up to the legacy that was left behind by Bob's passing. It was the only way I knew to honor my husband and carry on his life.

From We "to "I"

"Those we love don't go away;
they walk beside us every day."

- Anonymous

March 13, 2017 (Day 47)

During lunch break at work, we were talking about our upcoming spring break and everyone's plans. When I told them about my first vacation by myself, I kept using the word "we." I finally noticed the confusion after a co-worker asked me if I was going with a friend.

I did the same thing many years ago right after my husband and I got married, but back then I had a hard time saying "we" instead of "I." Now, it was the total opposite.

It didn't matter whether I liked it or not. I was doing things, making decisions by myself, and creating some new memories without my husband. But, in a way, he was always there with me whatever I was doing.

I said good morning to him every day. I could clearly see him in my mind. Before he passed, on weekdays, he would get up fifteen minutes before I did to cook breakfast for us and pack snacks for me. Then he kissed me and woke me up. On weekends, we loved to stay up late to catch up on some of our favorite TV shows. Sleeping in was a must for us. He usually pretended to still be sleeping when I woke up. I would pinch his nose and call him "lazy bones" in Chinese. He would say, "You are a big, lazy bones," in Chinese back to me. This was one of a few of the Chinese sentences that he knew how to say well. We loved to spoil each other, and we were never tired of those same old jokes.

Somethings will probably never change. When I get home every day, I still say, "I am home!" as I walk into the kitchen.

I still hear him saying, "Welcome home! How was your day?" I also say good night to him. My shoulders still remember the snuggled feeling from his big, warm hug.

Looking back, I clearly saw his influence in my life. With every decision I made after he passed away, his ideas and opinions were considered—from what to eat for dinner to where to go for a vacation. We *were* each other.

He took half of my life with him when he passed away. But he also left half of him with me. I was still a whole person. I just had a broken heart. He didn't break my heart, his departure did. Now I was starting to feel his love healing my wounds.

My First Birthday

Without My Husband

"It's hard to turn the page when you know someone won't be in the next chapter, but the story must go on."

\- By an Unknown Author

March 20, 2017 (Day 53)

Before I met my husband, birthdays were sad and torturous. My mom and dad never remembered my birthday, and I would wait for and wish for someone to simply say, "Happy birthday!" I hated birthdays. I honestly don't even remember how I spent my thirtieth birthday. I guess it was just another day; or maybe worse than a normal day because of the hope I had put into someone noticing.

My husband was so angry that I had been treated that way. He said he would make up for all the hard times I had; from then on, it would be only good times!

He followed through.

My husband planned a surprise birthday party in Shanghai for me for my thirty-first birthday, however, my best friend told me everything beforehand. My husband was mad at her for many years for ruining the surprise. It didn't matter to me. I received a lot of gifts for the first time in my whole life. We had a great dinner and wonderful time that day. Above all, the most amazing gift I received that day was to feel I was worth the effort and celebration.

My man always made every birthday of mine very special. Many people helped celebrate my first birthday in America. My in-laws and sisters-in-law called me and sang "Happy Birthday." My stepdaughter secretly baked my first homemade birthday cake. From that moment, I knew Bob had not only given me all of his love, he also gave me a family.

The highlight of all birthdays had to be my fortieth. This time, Bob finally pulled off his surprise party. He had gathered so many family and friends to surprise me when I walked in. He even had an impromptu comedy group involved. I certainly felt like I was the most spoiled wife in the world.

As my first birthday without my man approached, I was not sure what my day would look like. I wasn't even sure I wanted to celebrate it. It turned out to be a very fun birthday! Several weeks before, my stepdaughter and her fiancé had already demanded I leave that day unscheduled. Birthday morning, they came in while I was still in bed and cooked a delicious breakfast for me. Ashley made me wear a sparkly birthday crown and purple glitter birthday sash as she took me out for two surprise activities.

Our first activity was pottery making. I had always wanted to try this, but somehow just never did. The instructor had to do some quick operations to save my bowl, but I was pretty happy with the result. The second activity was painting. Bob and I had decided to go to Paris to celebrate when he beat the cancer. We hadn't been able to take that trip, so my stepdaughter arranged for us to paint the Eiffel Tower on canvases.

Overall, the first birthday without my husband was not bad. Bob is not physically here with me anymore, but I see him everywhere in my life. My stepkids all love cooking and enjoying life just like he did. My stepdaughter always takes care of me just as he did. My sisters-in-law call me or text me all the time just like he used to.

The only difference now is that he is not just one person; he is in many of us who loved him dearly.

The First Time Traveling Alone

"The secret to change is to focus all of your energy, not on fighting the old, but on building the new."

- Socrates

April 3, 2017 (Day 67)

My husband took care of everything when we traveled. My only job was to show up and be pretty. He encouraged me to pack many outfits that could be used later for my blog. In his backpack, there would be snacks, drinks, make-up touch-up essentials, a jacket, and a pair of flat shoes for me; he knew at some point I would want to ditch the heels.

This trip was a totally different story. The night before I left, I realized my small cross body bags were not as practical as I had thought. I went out and bought myself my very first backpack. Now that I had to carry everything, I packed light and gave up on heels and fancy dresses.

I had three goals for this trip: the first, was not to lose my phone or wallet, the second was not to get sick or hurt, and the last one was to enjoy myself. I knew my standards were low. I was quite nervous about this trip since I had been living in a bubble for the last ten years and treated like a princess. Now, I felt like I was lacking a lot of life skills. The night before I left, I was crying and really wished Bob were there with me.

My first flight from Detroit to LA was late, as we sat on the runway for forty-five minutes. I was told my second flight would wait for me. I ran from one terminal to another once we landed at LAX. When I finally got to the gate, it was closed. I was put on standby for four hours, where I literally stood by the flight podium for two hours, and still didn't get on the flight. Later, I had to fly to Vegas and then finally to Honolulu. My twelve-hour flight turned into a forty-hour nightmare. But, on day two, when I finally stepped into my hotel room, I opened the window and saw the ocean view and instantly felt everything had been worth it.

However, it turned out the bad luck was still with me on day three. I had booked an active volcano tour to the Big Island. In order to catch my flight, I had to get up at 4:00 a.m. I went downstairs to get myself a cup of coffee to get the day started. I sat on the shuttle bus and took a sip, my belly instantly felt as though it were burning. When I looked down, I saw that I had spilled my coffee.

Great! I never knew that I needed to double-check whether the cap was closed tightly. My husband had always handed me drinks; he would always make sure everything was okay before placing it in my hands. This was my once-in-a-lifetime opportunity to take some great photos from the helicopter flying over the volcanos and lava, and now my whole front was covered with coffee! I didn't get upset; I just told myself I needed to buy a T-shirt before I got into my chopper. Long story short, after many attempts, I finally got myself a tee and was ready to fly—then I was told the helicopter tour had to be cancelled due to the weather. What? I couldn't believe my luck!

Later, I went hiking in Volcano National Park with my tour group. Out of habit, I couldn't help but search for my man. There was nothing familiar around me, other than the sky. I suddenly missed his warm, thick hands. He had always held my hand wherever we went. We had hiked together a few times and had so much to talk and laugh about. But now it was just so quiet. At the end of the day, I finally saw lava and a place where the lava flowed into the ocean. Standing on the cliff alone, facing the ocean, I suddenly burst into tears. "We made it, Man," was all I could say at that moment.

On the way back to the airport, I sat alone and cried. Suddenly, familiar music started to play; it was one of our favorite songs, "Somewhere over the Rainbow" by Israel Kamakawiwo'Ole. I instantly smiled, even with tears still in my eyes. I knew that song was sent as my husband's way of trying to comfort me.

After those tough first three days, I decided I'd had enough. It was time for me to enjoy myself. I was on vacation, not in a prison, right? So, I did my homework and found some great restaurants and other activities to do. I finally hopped on a chopper to see the whole island of Oahu. Although it was not the lava view I had initially planned on, the experience was still amazing. I also had my first snorkeling experience. My real vacation had started. I was surprised that I was very happy eating dinner at a restaurant by myself. I initiated a lot of conversations with strangers, and I was so grateful because I had met so many great people on this trip.

The most important outcome from this trip was that I felt more confident. It was kind of like a test for me. When I am at home, I'm comfortable and I don't have a lot of difficult situations come up. But this trip showed me how things could go wrong. Luckily, I was able to manage everything and enjoyed myself. Now to plan my summer trip to Paris!

Live My Life Wide Open

"Live your life with arms wide open.
Today is where your book begins. The rest is still unwritten."

\- Natasha Bedingfield

April 14, 2017 (Day 78)

The first time I heard the catchphrase "Live your life wide open" for the Buick Cascade, I had to smile. It was such a positive and confident attitude toward life. I felt like my husband was still living through my body, my eyes, and my heart. Together we continue to live our life wide open.

I still have a responsibility to make sure we do all the things on our bucket list. I rode in a helicopter without doors on my vacation in Hawaii. It was scary, but it was so much fun. I don't know how to swim, and I am afraid of water, but I went snorkeling. I saw a big sea turtle and many beautiful fish. I like this "no door" philosophy now, it has opened my eyes to a much wider world.

The day before my spring break, one of my co-workers told me, "Enjoy your vacation! You will meet great people." He was right, I met many amazing people during my Hawaii trip. Every one of them taught me a life lesson.

When I was running between two terminals to find my gate, there was a lady who came to me and told me, "Don't worry. I will help you." She was pulling her own carry-on, but still ran with me and tried to calm me down. When we finally got to the gate, the airplane was there, but the door was closed. She argued with the staff on my behalf, telling them that she witnessed how hard I tried to make it, and they should reopen the door to let me in. I didn't get on my plane, but I was touched by how an absolute stranger would go through that much trouble to help me.

There was another lady who had missed the same flight. We were both on standby and decided to hang out together. We went to a bar at the airport, had some cocktails, and talked about life. Time goes super-fast when you have someone to talk to. She talked me into flying to Vegas with her and then on to Honolulu. We were both upset and tired, so we went to a different bar and continued our conversation, followed by more heart-to-heart talking, and finally we headed to Vegas. I can't imagine what my forty-hour trip would have looked like without her company and support. She left Honolulu one day before I did and sent me a message. "I am sitting in LAX now and waiting for my second flight. It seems like I will not miss it this time."

I booked a lot of tours while I was in Hawaii. During the Big Island tour, I met an older widow from Australia. Her husband had passed away eight months prior, and she was going on this trip for him, too. She was a such nice person, but she seemed so lonely all the time. I talked to her quite often, but I didn't have the ability to make her smile. It broke my heart when I saw her sitting among all the young kids at the airport. She just seemed so lost. She made me realize that my tough time was not really that bad. I couldn't imagine what would happen if I lost my man at her age. Would I be able to be happy and enjoy myself ever again?

I usually sat by myself on the tour buses, but there was a young girl who asked me if she could sit next to me when we were on our way to a luau. She was a senior college student from Florida, majoring in journalism. She was also a travel blogger! She showed me some breathtaking photos she had taken earlier that morning. She and some friends she had met on the trip illegally climbed a mountain to watch the sunrise. She told me how dangerous that hike was, but how rewarding the views were. She reminded me of myself when I was younger. I was so brave and didn't mind taking risks. It had seemed like the whole world belonged to me to explore and to conquer. I was hoping it wasn't too late.

Later that evening at the luau, I was sitting across from another young girl at a long table. We started talking, and she introduced me to her brother. My husband often comes up in my conversations with whomever I talk to. I just naturally remember what he once said or did. Anyway, I don't remember how, but I mentioned my husband while I was talking to Rebekah. So, she asked me, "Where is your husband?" I instantly teared up and told her about my man.

Then the host asked all the honeymooners and those who were celebrating anniversaries to come to the stage. There were a few couples who were celebrating fifty years of marriage. The host said some tender words, and the music was very touching. I wandered to a dark corner and cried. My husband and I had planned to be together for at least thirty or forty years, even with our difference in age. My man had tried so hard to stay with me longer.

At that moment, I felt somebody pat my back. It was Rebekah asking, "Are you okay? Do you want to go to the back with us?" Rebekah and her brother, David, were standing at the back of the crowd so they could see better. It felt so good to know, even in a strange place, there was someone who cared about me.

On the way back to our hotels, Rebekah and I sat together and talked. Before we said goodbye, she invited me to have brunch with them the next day. We had a great time.

She asked if I would like to join them to see the sunset on the beach that evening. I thought, *Why not?* I hung out with them again, and we found a rooftop bar next to the beach. We sat there talking and listening to the island music. They were such nice people with warm hearts. I loved to listen to their stories and was especially impressed by something that Rebekah said: "There are a lot of girls who just can't live alone. So, they feel they need a man."

I like to hang out with wise people; I can learn from them.

Later, we found out we were on the same plane back to LA, so we hung out again on the last day. We went to the flea market and just strolled on the streets to enjoy the wonderful Hawaii weather and views before we left. We still stay in touch.

My biggest lesson: Live your life wide open so you can meet great people, try new things, and grow wiser!

It's Okay to Not Be Okay

"Don't be ashamed to weep; 'tis right to grieve. Tears are only water, and flowers, trees, and fruit cannot grow without water. But there must be sunlight also. A wounded heart will heal in time, and when it does, the memory and love of our lost ones is sealed inside to comfort us."

- Brian Jacques

April 21, 2017 (Day 85)

While I was talking with a new friend about my Hawaii trip, she suddenly asked me, "Were you scared of traveling alone?"

Pausing, I answered, "Of course, I was." I was surprised by the question. This conversation made me realize that I need to share the whole story; not just the brave and pretty parts.

I never intended to be brave or to be an inspiration. Really, I would rather be someone who still has loving parents and a loving spouse, but it seems I am out of luck in that department. Life keeps testing me, and I am trying to survive. I'm often scared, sad, angry, and confused--and I cry--just like everybody else who is going through the grieving process.

I purposely blocked out the last week of my husband's life from my memory. It was just too painful to think about. Someday, I will revisit those dark days when I feel I am ready. But not yet. I still lay my head on his ashes box and imagine it is his warm chest. I cried four days in a row while I cleaned up my husband's car and traded it in. I even cried at the dealership. I'm pretty sure I thoroughly scared the sales guy.

I cried for more than half an hour the night before my trip to Hawaii. I was scared because I had never traveled alone in this country. I was also very sad because Bob had always wanted to show me Hawaii. Now I was going on my own. The first three days of that trip I cried *a lot.*

The day I arrived back home; I opened a package I had received from my family. I was crying instantly again. It was an amazing painting of my man. The painting looked so real. His facial expression was just so lively; it's like he was right there looking at me. I cried even as I wrote about it.

Hopefully you've noticed the millions of times I have used the word "cry." Okay, a million might be an exaggeration, but it's a lot. My point is that it is okay to not be okay for a while. It's okay--this is the new normal for me after my husband passed away.

I am scared; I struggle; I cry quite often. I give myself permission to sometimes not be okay, even cry in public if I need to.

I don't think crying is a sign of weakness; it is a way of surviving for me. Just as you sweat when you're running, I sometimes cry just to survive. I cry because I need to let it all out so I will have the ability to move forward.

Ten Years in America

*"We cannot tell what may happen to us in the strange medley of
life. But we can decide what happens in us
—how we can take it, what we do with it —
and that is what really counts in the end."*

- Joseph Fort Newton

April 28, 2017 (Day 92)

April 19th is just a normal day for most people, but for me it is a life-changing date that I will remember forever. Ten years ago, on that date, I came to America and started my new life in Michigan. I was shocked when I stepped out of the airport. I couldn't read any signs on the road, and I couldn't understand anything people were saying to me. I was totally lost. But I knew I had my man, and he would be my bridge to this whole new world. As long as I had him, I was not afraid.

Bob and I met in Shanghai. I knew no English and he only could say, "hi," "goodbye," "thank you," and "beer," in Chinese (this may or may not be an improvement over my stepdaughter who to this day knows "melon," "watermelon," "cantaloupe," and "hi."").

Through body language and a handy dictionary, we felt we had known each other for our whole lives. We knew what the other was thinking and we were always so happy to be together. Ten years ago, I gave up my career, my friends, and my life in Shanghai and came here to marry my man.

Now he is gone. As you can imagine, I was quite blue and unsure of what I wanted to do a few days prior to April 19th to commemorate the day. I wanted to be happy and celebrate, but I really wanted to do it with him, just like the past nine years.

Traditionally, my husband and I always went to a Mexican restaurant to honor this anniversary. You may ask, "Why a Mexican restaurant? Why not a Chinese or American restaurant?" It goes back ten years to that day. After over thirty hours of flights from China, I was super tired, and maybe a little grumpy. My man knew I would not like the American version of Chinese food, and I was not yet a fan of any Western food. He really wanted to find something that I could enjoy, so he came up with what he thought was a great idea. He figured since Chinese and Mexicans both like rice, I must like Mexican food.

Mexican food is very rare in China. The closest thing that I had ever had to Mexican food was Taco Bell in Shanghai. I can honestly tell you, the dinner my first day was a disaster. It was so bad, in fact, I was worried that I may starve to death in this country. We have often laughed at the memory of that day. Every year on April 19th, since that day, we have eaten Mexican food to celebrate my first day in America.

I was quite sad the night before this milestone day, but I didn't want to cry because I didn't want puffy eyes for the next day. This April 19th was going to be unique and special. I was going to meet Stacy London. Stacy was the host for the TV show, *What Not to Wear*, and had been my style inspiration for years. I really didn't want big, puffy eyes for such a special day. I was working on my computer, when suddenly my calendar popped up and with the notification: *Ten years ago tomorrow Grace came to America.* It was the reminder my man had set on his phone, and since we shared our calendar, it popped up for me.

This finally triggered my tears. I cried for about an hour. I was so angry at whoever was responsible for taking my man away from me. *Why me? Why him? Why us?* I was also very sad because he would have been so proud of me for getting the chance to meet with Stacy London.

I posted my ten-year anniversary on my social media early that morning. I was surprised to see a lot of people sending me congratulations. I was thinking: *What can I be congratulated about?* I came to this country to marry my husband, and now he has passed away.

Later that day, I finally realized it was a day that I needed to celebrate, even without him. I had achieved a lot in the last decade. I found my true love and was married, had my first house, learned English, how to drive, and a lot about American culture. I had my own family and received my teaching certificate and a full-time teaching job. I became a blogger and a TV co-host. Although my man has passed away, I am still holding my head high and chasing my fashion dream.

Once I made the decision to honor my accomplishments, my tenth anniversary of moving to America turned out to be one of the greatest days of my life. I hung out with Stacy London for the whole afternoon. I also met a new friend, Inez, a fellow blogger in Michigan. Inez and I even went to my favorite Mexican restaurant for dinner. We were talking about our lives and sipping margaritas. Life was still great!

Ten years down, with many more great years to come!

Learning to Live Alone

"If you want to be happy, learn to be alone without being lonely.
Learn that being alone does not mean being unhappy.
The world is full of plenty of interesting and
enjoyable things to do and people who can enrich your life."
- Michael Josephson

May 5, 2017 (Day 99)

Before my husband passed away, I broke down in tears many times because I highly doubted that I could live without him. Bob was my soulmate, my best friend. He was my everything, literally. He was my driver because driving made me very nervous. He was my cook because with a full-time job and almost full-time blogging, I barely had time to eat. He was the bag carrier when I went shopping. He did the laundry, vacuumed the house, and bought the groceries. He did just about everything so I could focus on my job and my dream.

I was very lucky, and I was spoiled! But the result of such extravagant love was that I was almost handicapped when it came to basic life skills. After my man passed away, I had to learn how to fill up my gas tank; he had always taken care of it. I learned how to order food and use a drive-through. I even learned how to write a check. After two weeks of the recycling guys refusing to take my recycling, I learned how to properly break down boxes and separate the paper from the plastics.

I know it sounds ridiculous, but this was my reality for the first three months after his passing. Luckily, I was a fast learner, and everything came under control rather quickly. I cooked myself a very healthy breakfast every morning. I packed healthy snacks for myself every day. I drove everywhere by myself with my GPS. I paid bills on time and never ran out of gas. I went to Hawaii by myself and then booked a trip to Paris. I learned how to deal with the pool repair people, the roof people, the lawn people, and the plumber. I am pretty proud of the results of my bargaining skills. The roof people had seen my shoe collection, so it made it pretty difficult, but I won.

I was very lucky that my stepdaughter and her fiancé visited me almost every weekend. They did so much for me – everything from cooking delicious dinners, pulling the weeds in my stubborn backyard, taking my blog photos, proofreading my posts, and driving me to some fashion events. They helped me understand financial and medical files. They even changed out my kitchen faucet. (I discovered my stepdaughter uses the same language my husband did when things don't go right; it must run in the family.) I knew they had their own life and I needed to learn how to handle everything by myself.

All the physical things were easy to learn and to adapt to. The hardest part was the absence of my husband's love and his companionship. It took me a long time to get used to eating alone. I still hate it, but I am doing it. My husband and I used to talk about everything. We always had so much to share and giggle about. Now that I don't have him, I talk to family and friends more often. Sometimes, I even talk to myself. Hey, sometimes I just need an expert's advice (My husband used to use that line when I caught him talking to himself!). It was hard after a long working day to walk into an empty house. (And I was not ready for a pet. My two granddogs visited every weekend.) To fix the loneliness, the first thing I did when I arrived home was to turn on my music.

It was just the beginning of learning to live alone. I still had a *looooong* way to go. One step at a time, that was all I took. I started buying myself flowers. I cooked more dinners for myself. I began plans to redecorate my house during my summer break to change things up a bit. I thought about hosting some dinner parties in the summer as well.

This house used to be a fun house. I was determined that this tradition continued.

Mother's Day

"You don't just complete my dad's life.
You add a special touch to mine, too."

- Anonymous

May 19, 2017 (Day 113)

Several weeks before my husband passed away, we came home with a new estimate for how much time was left for my man. The estimates were just getting shorter and shorter. I was trying very hard to be normal. But seeing how hard eating became for him (one of his favorite activities) and how he became nauseous, I couldn't help but burst into tears. I just repeated, "I don't want you to die."

Bob always hugged me and said, "You will be fine. It will be very difficult, but you will be fine."

I highly doubted this, and said, "You don't understand; I can't live without you. I will just kill myself."

My husband held my head up and looked into my eyes. "Have you ever thought about how Ashley would feel if you killed yourself? How devastated she would be?"

I suddenly calmed down and woke up from my anger and selfishness. He was right. It didn't matter what happened. As long as I was alive, this was still the home for my family. I had a responsibility to take care of them for my man and for myself. This was partially because my family had been taking very good care of me since the first day I came to

America. I was lucky enough to celebrate Mother's Day, too, even if I didn't have my own kids.

Ashley and her fiancé (who has been around almost as long as I have) always brought a card, flowers, and a gift. This year, they secretly came to my house, pulled weeds, and put down four yards of mulch in my garden while I was out. When I came home, they were almost done. They also brought me a very cute hanging strawberry pot. They knew how much I love gardening.

There were a lot of times I felt guilty because I didn't feel I deserved the honor of being considered a mother. When I came to the family, Ashley had already graduated from college and my stepson had already finished his first year of college. I hadn't changed a single diaper, but I get the benefit of being a mother figure in our family. My man used to say, "They may never call you "Mom," but you are the mom for them. They know you are taking care of them, and you are here for them."

On this Mother's Day morning, I received an unpleasant comment on my Facebook post. A lady said I didn't really miss my husband, I just missed a maid and complained about how much work I had to do without him. I knew these types of comments would eventually happen since I had put myself out there in the public domain, but it still hurt when I read those cold-hearted words. I told Ashley about the comment and she was quite angry. She looked into that lady's profile and asked if she could respond to her. Her fiancé even jokingly asked where she lived. Of course, I told them there was no need to get into an argument over online comments, but their response felt so good because they were willing to protect me and fight for me.

There were quite a few people who asked me if I would move back to China after my husband passed away.

Each time I heard it I wondered why they were asking me this weird question. Later, I realized that they knew I came to America to marry my husband. Now that he was gone, they felt there would be no purpose for me to stay in a foreign country anymore.

But what they didn't know was that my husband did not just give me unconditional true love; he gave me a family here, and for them I would stay.

Feeling Loved

"Where there is love there is life."

- Mahatma Gandhi

May 26, 2017 (Day 120)

On the way to work one morning, the car in front of me caught my attention. I couldn't see who was in the passenger seat, but what I could see was the guy sitting in the driver's seat trying to adjust the sun visor of the passenger side to block the morning sun. He did it a few times and kept turning right to check if it needed more adjustment.

I smiled and teared up. I smiled because I saw love, a lot of deep love in that small action. It showed how much he deeply cared about the person in the passenger seat. He wanted to make sure that person was comfortable and happy. I wondered who that lucky person was. His wife? His kid? His parents? Or maybe his dog?

My husband used to do this simple gesture for me all the time. We took long road trips almost every year. Somehow, the car ride always made me sleepy. I usually kicked the seat back and took a nap. My man always switched the music to the spa channel to help me relax. He would also adjust the sun visor if the sun was in my eyes. Sometimes, he even added a map or newspaper to the sun visor to create a bigger shadow for me. Love is in all of those little tiny details, right?

Every day I miss my man's love terribly. This grieving journey has been very painful and difficult, but at the same time it has also been enlightening. It made me look at the world from a slightly different point of view. I started to notice there were many different types of love in my life now, and I still feel loved even without my husband.

The departure of my husband didn't cut off the connection I had with my amazing stepdaughter and her fiancé; instead it strengthened our bonding as a family. One weekend, they put four more yards of mulch in my yard and even worked through the rain. My school and my co-workers were super supportive, too. I always felt safe and comfortable talking to anyone about work or personal problems. Some of them even became my photographer to help me with my blog photos.

Even my students adored me very much! Just like my man, my students thought my Chinese accent was quite cute. They often tricked me into saying words like "vowel" or "further." After I said those words, they would say, "It is so cute!" I guess when someone really loves you, even the flaws are cute.

Most of my eighth graders refer to me as their "School Mom." One Sunday, I even went out with one of my former students for lunch. She was in her third year of college and became an entrepreneur. She used to say I was her second mom.

I also received many nice comments on my blog and social media posts every day. I knew everyone was super busy with their own life, but they made time to read my posts and leave very long and thoughtful comments. That meant so much to me, especially those "friends" whom I've never met before in real life and maybe will never meet in this lifetime. But they are always there for me.

Every time I felt lost, confused, and didn't know how I could go through another day, the unconditional love from all of the people in my life reminded me how lucky I was. Their love has always lifted me up!

My Husband's First Birthday After He Passed Away

"If tears could build a stairway, and memories a lane,
I'd walk right up to Heaven and bring you home again."
- Author unknown

June 2, 2017 (Day 127)

Special days bring so much pain to those who have lost their loved ones. About a week before my husband's first birthday since he had passed away, I started having another very difficult time. A couple of days before his birthday, my emotions took over completely. I was crying the whole way home from work while I was driving. It was rainy, and the traffic was quite bad. I knew it was dangerous, but I just couldn't hold it in or control it anymore.

Based on my four-month grieving experience, I knew I needed to find a way to save myself before I went too far into a depression. I had a few morning pep talks on the way to work, but those only cheered me for a short time. I tried many things that had worked for me before, but somehow this time they just couldn't fix it. I really missed him, so I went on to his Facebook.

I was crying even harder when I started to read. Something unexpectedly happened as I continued to read.

"Some quality hammock time on the last Friday in August. Oh, yes I did!"

On May 28, 2016, his birthday, just after the first type of chemo failed and the tumors came back crazy fast and big, he said:

"Thanks very much for all the birthday wishes! I'm in such a good mood I'm giving you all Monday off, with pay!"

That day was Memorial Day.

I started to laugh, louder and louder. Yes! That was my man.

My stepdaughter booked us a weekend camping trip long before he had passed away to celebrate my husband's birthday. To celebrate his birthday, we went camping; without him. We barely mentioned him while we were at the campground. Everybody had had a few hard days, so we just enjoyed each other's company. We had a delicious campfire dinner, walked in the rain, ate s'mores, and played *Uno*. There was a short toast, and we shared a bottle of wine. Just like the good ol' days.

The next day was Memorial Day. My father-in-law and brother-in-law, both military veterans, were the co-grand marshals for the parade. Our big family all came to support them as well. While listening to the speech, I was thinking of my husband. He had been my hero. He kept his positive spirit all the way till the end. He never shed one tear during this whole journey. He left so much for us. I was sad. He was too. But he chose to really enjoy every minute of his life that he had left.

And so, I came to believe, so should I!

On the way back home, I discarded my GPS and took some back roads I had never been on before. There were many lakes and beautiful houses along the way. My smile grew bigger and bigger. I suddenly noticed that I loved driving on winding roads; it was so much fun! I really understood why my husband always loved to travel. It was pretty cool to get lost in a totally strange place and just enjoy the unfamiliar scenery.

Life was good again, and I vowed to remember to enjoy every little thing that makes me happy.

Happy birthday, my man, and thank you very much for saving me again!

My Speech for My Husband's Memorial Party

"I love you not only for what you are, but for what I am
when I am with you. I love you not only for what you have
made of yourself, but for what you are making of me.
I love you for the part of me that you bring out."

- Roy Croft

June 17, 2017 (Day 142)

The big party for my husband was just a day away. I had asked a few family and friends to give short speeches during the party. Being his wife, I really needed say something too, but I had no way of carrying out this speech without breaking down. So, I wrote it in my blog:

"Bob was a man nobody can replace, at least not in my heart. He was often mad the last few months of his life and asked me, 'Why can we only have ten years together?'

I didn't know the answer. The only thing I know is Bob and I were perfect for each other, and we had such a happy life together. Even during the darkest time in our life, we still managed to truly enjoy every minute of each other's company, support, and love.

For others, my man may have been just an ordinary guy, but for me he was the best husband and my best friend.

He taught me so many things, like how to speak English and drive a car. He taught me to simply enjoy the small things in our lives, like: grabbing a big Slurpee for a road trip, barbecuing over charcoal in our backyard, holding a beer in his hand, and telling his cool jokes with friends at our parties or jumping in the pool like a cannon ball. He had the ability to make everybody laugh. He was such a fun guy to be around, and certainly, he lived his life the best way he could, with no regrets.

Marrying my man was the best decision I ever made in my life. I am grateful for every minute we had together. We used to tell each other how lucky we were to be husband and wife. We had ten truly joyful years with the deepest love, happiest marriage, and most trusted partnership that anyone could imagine.

He gave me the experience of being deeply understood, truly supported, and unconditionally loved.

When I got upset, he stayed calm and helped me calm down. When I was worried, he reminded me how much I/we had accomplished. When I wasn't sure what to do, he figured it out.

The past five months have been a true testimony of how much he left for us. People have often told me I am very strong, but the truth is I am carrying on all his love and that is why I am so brave. His love for life is already deeply rooted in our hearts. We may not have the quick wit he had, but we are all trying to pull a joke when we can. We may not always have the positive outlook he had, but we are trying to have more faith and believe everything will work out.

So, today, let's all use the best way Bob knew how to celebrate and have a toast for my man and celebrate his life!

Ten-Year Wedding Anniversary... Without Him

"Death leaves a heartache no one can heal;
love leaves a memory no one can steal."
- From a headstone in Ireland

June 18, 2017 (Day 143)

Here's a letter I wrote to my man on our anniversary:

Hello Man,

How is your new life in heaven? Is every day just like vacation? I can imagine you are either holding your beer and joking around with your old and new friends or napping on the beach. I know you would rather have stayed with me, with our family.

We used to send emails to each other all the time when we first met many years ago. Do you remember? I am still surprised that you could stand my horrible grammar and broken sentences. You were always so patient with me and never showed any frustration with my limited English.

Through those letters, we came to know each other. I felt I had already known you for my whole life from the very beginning of our relationship. For our ten-year wedding anniversary on June 18, I decided to write you a letter, just like before.

Right after you passed away, your sister, Penny, thanked me very much for making you the happiest man on Earth for the past ten years. I told her those ten years were the best time of my life as well. There were so many evenings we were having delicious dinners, drinking wine, holding hands, and telling each other how lucky we both were to be husband and wife. Yes, we were quite cheesy.

Man, thank you so much for surprising me by having my Chinese friend show up on our wedding day. You knew that none of my side of the family could make it to our wedding, and you wanted to bring a little bit of China home to me in America. You tried so hard to invite our Chinese friends to our wedding in America. You were always so good at surprising me, like the big surprise party on my fortieth birthday. I planned to give you one this year on your birthday as well, but I didn't get the chance.

I am doing okay. Most days I am pretty good, but there are other days when I am a hot mess. Can you believe I cried at work a few days ago? I have never done that before in my whole life. I guess now I have a new record. I am trying very hard to keep our little house and big yard in order. We got a new roof and our pool got a new surface. Now, we are all working on your life celebration party as you requested. I know there must be a lot of beer, wine, and laughter. No tears. I will remember, sir.

Everyone says the first year of being a widow is the hardest. I am not even halfway there yet, so I don't really know. But I do know it sucks, and I am very good at crying in public now. Do you remember how I used to have trouble crying? It certainly is not the case anymore. I have become an expert at crying in recent months.

There are many milestones in the first year of being alone and I have survived—Valentine's Day, my birthday, the anniversary I came to America to marry you, and your birthday. Now our wedding anniversary is upon me. I have no clue what I am going to do without you and how big of a mess I will be. But I will live. Wish me luck, Man!

I miss you sooooo much and love you forever!

Your troubled wife,
Grace

Surviving the
First Wedding Anniversary

"Attitude is a choice. Happiness is a choice. Optimism is a choice. Kindness is a choice. Giving is a choice. Respect is a choice. Whatever choice you make makes you. Choose wisely."
- Roy T. Bennett, The Light in the Heart

June 18, 2017 (Day 143)

A few months before my husband passed away, we had a special conversation regarding his funeral arrangements. In his written wishes, he had already stated that he didn't want a traditional funeral; instead he wanted a big happy party. He was quite excited about the idea and said that it would be so cool that all of his family and friends would come together, hold drinks, and talk about his quick wit and the countless cool jokes he had made.

To honor his wish, we decided to host this party on June 18th, our ten-year wedding anniversary. We later realized that the same day was also Father's Day, so we switched the date to the 17th. The preparation for this party started in April. We had gotten a new roof, repaired the pool, put six trucks of mulch in the yard, and planted a big container garden around the pool and patio. The theme for his party was "Travel Around the World." So, the decorations, eating utensils, food, and drinks all followed this theme.

The weather called for 50% rain that day, but I knew my man would find a way to avoid it. He loved parties and certainly would not ruin his own. There were nearly a hundred people who showed up, and everyone had a great time. There were seven people who gave speeches about my man, some from his work, some family, and some lifelong friends. The speeches had to be my favorite moments – listening to all the funny stories about my husband. Sometimes, I envy how he touched so many people's lives and left such a positive mark.

The success of my husband's life celebration party was the best gift on our tenth wedding anniversary and felt like medicine to my broken heart. After everyone left my house, I was so tired, but finally felt some relief. I cried, laughed, and talked to my man's memory book and his ashes. I told him we did it. As promised, we gave him the best celebration party we could. He deserved it.

After several months of dealing with grief, I knew I should ask for help when I needed it. About a week before our wedding anniversary, I messaged my stepdaughter and told her I should not be alone that day. That was her first Father's Day without her dad, too, so, we kind of really needed each other's company. We had dim sum for brunch and Korean BBQ for dinner. We even shared a whole bottle of Korean liquor.

The first wedding anniversary after my man passed away turned out to be a pretty good day, and I didn't even cry. There were choices I had to make every day and I chose to make happy choices, as my man would. I appreciate the wonderful times my man and I shared, and I will carry on the positive outlook as long as I can.

My Solo Trip

to Paris, Part-1

"Don't look for me, just go see the world
and create your own memories."
- Robert Buck

July 14, 2017 (Day 168)

Bob and I had a bucket list that we had created a few years before he passed. Paris was on the top of the list.

In the summer of 2010, we spent several weeks in Munich, Germany. What a great home base for exploring the Alps and beyond! I had always dreamt of seeing and smelling the lavender fields in the Provence region of France.

Unfortunately, it was still a dream as we got there about two weeks too late! Timing really *is* everything! We still made the best of the trip and visited Lyon on our way to the beaches of Cannes before heading back to Munich. The concierge at our hotel had directed us to a small hidden gem of a restaurant in the old part of Lyon. I'll never forget walking along the narrow stone streets, around this corner and that, to arrive at the open-walled eatery. It was decorated in rich, dark wood and heavy, soft velvet curtains. Mmm, the wine, the croissants, the roast duck...*heavenly!*

Fast forward to a few months before my man passed away; we talked about all the places we had been to and where we really wanted to go next. He said if he could pull through this time, we would go to Paris and then go to see the lavender. A few weeks before his departure, he said, "You may have to go to Paris without me."

I was trying to put on a brave face and joke around by saying, "Sure, I will send you postcards." But tears were already all over my face. I told him I would look for him wherever I went. He held my head to his chest and said, "Don't look for me, just go see the world and create your own memories."

So, I went to Paris alone. I thought about staying there longer and visiting Provence to see the lavender. At the last minute, I decided not to be so ambitious.

Before I left for the trip, so many people told me not to go. I did not speak or understand French, and I had never traveled internationally alone. My family doctor even yelled at me, "Have you watched the movie *Taken II?* Have you seen the news about those crazy terrorists?"

The night before my flight, I was stopped at a red light and randomly turned my head to my left. The sign on the theater building said, "Paris can wait." Was it a warning sign sent to me by my man? It made me nervous. I still went. On the way to the airport, I gave my stepdaughter directions about how to handle certain things - just in case!

I had fully prepared myself that this might not be an easy trip. When I traveled to Hawaii alone in March, it took me more than thirty hours to get to Honolulu. So, I packed enough things just in case I had to spend the night at the airport in NYC. The first flight was on time (yes!). As the second flight was boarding on time I thought, *maybe I am lucky this time.* Everyone on that plane was so friendly and someone helped me put my heavy carry-on into the overhead bin. The older gentleman who sat next to me said he had been to Paris many times and gave me quite a bit of info.

At end of the conversation he said, "You will love Paris, and you will meet a lot of people, especially a lot of men. They love beautiful women."

Pairs, here I come!

My Solo Trip

to Paris, Part-2

"Traveling solo does not always mean you're alone.
Most often, you meet marvelous people along
the way and make connections that last a lifetime."

- Jacqueline Boone

July 21, 2017 (Day 175)

The flight to Paris was no problem at all, but it took quite a while to go through customs. The young officer behind the booth was quite serious. I have read sometimes they give Asian people a hard time. I put on my big smile, and said, "Bonjour!" I saw his frozen face melt a little bit. "That is the only word I can say in French," I continued with an even bigger smile.

He stamped my passport while smiling, and suddenly, "Ni Hao!" I laughed so hard. He had just said "hi" to me in Chinese. Peace starts with a smile.

I had lived up to my intention and good things happened. For this trip, I decided I would initiate conversations instead of waiting on others to talk to me first. Throughout the trip I met so many great people and made some new friends.

During the Notre Dame tour, I met two ladies from Georgia. We had lunch together, an afternoon snack and drinks, and then dinner. We were sitting at the restaurant for more than six hours chatting and laughing. You know the feeling when you instantly click with someone? It was like we had known each other for a long time. I told them I felt like my husband had sent two sisters to me to accompany me on my adventure. They invited me to continue the trip with them throughout the rest of Europe. I was seriously considering joining them, but later I had to say no since I didn't pack any extra medicine with me. Bummer!

Then, I met a beautiful girl at breakfast in my hotel. She was German and lived in London. We went shopping together after breakfast and scored a few vintage scarfs with great deals. She helped me take photos and was a very honest shopping buddy too. With her help I found the best white bow tie button down shirt. Now, I know, if I go to London someday, I will have a friend there.

When I was in the Chanel store near my hotel, I was looking for someone to take a photo of me. I asked a very pretty Asian girl who just happened to be standing next to me. She looked at me and asked, "Are you asking to take a photo with me?"

I said, "No, I hope you can take a photo of me." I heard a group of people near her laugh very hard. She took a few photos of me and then walked away. I asked the laughing people what was so funny. It turned out to be Kimberley Anne Woltemas, quite a big celebrity with almost six million followers on Instagram. I felt pretty bad, so I waited for her to finish her own photo shoot and took a photo with her.

It was as if my husband was everywhere with me, enjoying every minute of this journey. When I was in the gardens at Versailles, suddenly some old memories came back to me. We had gone to a very similar palace in Germany seven years ago, and of course, we had a great time there. I was crying by myself and talking to him in my mind for a while. I know, if he were still here, he would give me a bear hug, rub my head, and tell me how sorry he was. I treated myself to a nice dinner to make up for my bad mood later.

I was happy and sad at the same time to see one of the bars offer Paulaner beer. My husband and I met at Shanghai Paulaner, so I had to have a beer to honor him.

This whole trip was so smooth and filled with amazing moments. I loved every day sitting outside of a restaurant, drinking my wine, eating delicious food, and people watching. Bob always wanted to show me the world and now he would be very proud of me. I have to say I am more confident after this trip.

Just an FYI, I didn't meet any man during this trip as the man on the plane had predicted.

The Six-Month Mark

"Home is any four walls that enclose the right person."
- Helen Rowland

July 28, 2017 (Day 182)

I wanted a home so badly when I was younger, but I never really had one to go back to or get support from. I had many extremely lonely and insecure years when I was in my twenties. It wasn't until I married Bob that I slowly experienced what a home is. His unconditional love helped me finally feel safe, relaxed, and happy.

My dad was the only one who cared about me, even just a little bit, when I was young. It was two months before my high school graduation when he passed away. My school required all students must stay at the dorm to focus on our studies; we were only allowed to go home twice a month. The last year of his life I hardly spent any time with him. I didn't even get a chance to see him when he passed away. When I got home, he was already in the coffin. I frequently had a dream about him. He was always walking away, and I would chase him, asking him why he didn't come home anymore––but he just kept walking away, and I was always crying when I woke up.

After I met my man, if I were crying in a dream, no matter how deeply he was sleeping, he always came to me and held me in his arms while patting me on my back.

After Bob passed, he had come to my dreams a few times; it was always lighthearted, continuing as we had always been, laughing and playful. Then one time, it was really difficult. In my dream, he was dying. At the last moment, I was holding his hand, and he used his last breath to mumble, "I love you." I woke up with tears streaming down my face. It was about two o'clock in the morning as I sat alone in my bed crying. This time, he was not here to hold me; instead, he was the one who had made me cry.

The next day, I texted my best friend and told her that I should not be alone at the six-month anniversary of Bob's death. She replied, "I am here for you and that day is yours." We went for some retail therapy, had a nice dinner, and spent some lovely time on her back patio with a fire in the fire pit and glasses of wine in our hands. Of course, I cried again, but most of the time I was grateful. That morning, when I opened the windows at home, the air was very crisp, my garden was full of flowers, and the sky was so blue. I said aloud, "Thank you, Man, for giving me this beautiful home."

My heart had never found a home until I met Bob. I always believed that home was where he was. But I suddenly realized that I can be my own home. I told him many times before he passed away that there was no way I could live without him. Now, a half-year later, I was living and doing pretty well without him. It was not because I had moved on. I had just moved forward. He planted the seed of life. During the ten years of our marriage, he somehow trained me well in the ability to simply enjoy being alive.

What Death

Has Taught Me

*"Every man's life ends the same way. It is only the details of how
he lived and how he died that distinguish one man from another."*

\- Ernest Hemingway

August 4, 2017 (Day 189)

When I was younger, I never thought about death. It just seemed so far, far away. Then my dad passed away and now my husband too. These deaths of my loved ones were a wake-up call. They have certainly changed and shaped my life. I have even had my own near-death experience.

The day after I came back from Paris, it was about ninety degrees and my pool looked amazing. The solo trip had given me so much confidence, and I felt that there was nothing I could not handle. So, I decided to go swimming alone. One thing you need to know about this, I don't really know how to raise my head above the water to breath, so my style of swimming is to hold my breath while doing the strokes.

My man had bought me a few diving toys years ago to help me practice. I threw them into the shallow end of the pool, just like we used to do. The water was a little chilly but felt really good. I did a little bit of a warm-up and then swam from the shallow end to the deep end; it is about eight or nine feet deep in the deep end. I opened my eyes while still swimming under water, grabbed the edge of the deep end to stop myself, and then poked my head out to breathe.

I was a little bit out of breath, but I was feeling quite good. After a short break, I swam back to the shallow end. By that time, all the diving toys were slowly moving to the deep end, drawn by the filter. I knew there was no way I could dive that deep to get them out. So, I dove to the middle section of the pool to rescue them before they went too far. I picked up one, and then tried to pick up the second one. I suddenly lost my balance and felt as I was being pulled into the deeper end.

I am only five feet tall, so I was completely under the water. I saw a beautiful blue sky and the air bubbles from my mouth through a few feet of water above me. I needed to land somewhere so I could position myself and start the swimming strokes. So, I stopped panicking and struggling, and just stayed still. My toes felt the bottom of the pool, but it was not enough to kick myself up and poke my head out of the water. My legs and arms were moving very fast, but I was going nowhere. One thought alone was vivid in my mind. *This is not a joke, not a dream, I may die today in my own backyard.*

I continued struggling under the water. Somehow, I turned my head and I saw three small steps on the wall. I suddenly remembered that they were there for the diving board that used to be on the pool, but they were still quite far from me. I used all my strength to paddle and, finally, I reached the lowest step. When I poked my head out of the water, I realized how good it felt to be able to breathe again.

After a hot shower, I was drying myself, patted my belly and said, "I almost lost you today. I need to take better care of you from now on." That was the true awakening moment for me. Since that day, I have been cooking myself healthy meals, and make sure I don't stay up late. I even started my gym journey to get healthier. I spend more time with family and friends. I discovered that I *really* love people. I love talking to others, even strangers, and listening to their stories.

So, what has death taught me? I think I finally understand how to live in the present and simply enjoy what I have at this moment in my life—a sunny day, my beautiful gardens, a beautiful song, good food, good company and a good time. I am not going to kill my health anymore like I used to just to chase after my dream. Life has shown me that every breath could be my last.

Cooking for Myself

*"Cooking for others, for your loved ones, is pure joy.
Cooking for yourself is where the true self-love begins."*

- Grace Liang

August 11, 2017 (Day 196)

I hated cooking for myself when I was young and alone in Shanghai. I didn't even know how to cook. Seriously, I lived on carry-outs and leftovers. Most days, I would only eat two meals and some days it would be only one. When Bob and I were dating, he came to Shanghai to visit me. I was trying to show him that I could be a good wife. I bought a bag of frozen meals at the supermarket and cooked for him. Don't ask for the details; just let me tell you that was the end of my cooking career. My man was a great cook, and he promised that he would cook for us from that day forward.

I tried cooking again after I moved to America to marry my man. It started about a week after I arrived, I was seriously thinking that I would end up starving to death. At that time, I *really* didn't like any American food. This forced me to cook Chinese food. I guess many years of eating at restaurants helped me develop some cooking sense. Surprisingly, my cooking turned out to be quite good. I never even knew I had it in me. I guess when I cooked with love, everything turned out to be great.

Cooking for us, for our family and friends, holds some of the warmest memories of the last ten years. My late husband loved my Chinese cooking, and he was very proud of me for becoming a great cook. When I first heard the saying, "Cook up a storm," I was laughing so hard because that was totally my style of cooking. Usually after I cooked, our kitchen was a disaster—dirty pots and pans everywhere, the stove top covered with oil, spices, and pieces of food. I cooked well, I said nothing about cleaning.

My man was the biggest fan of my cooking. I never followed a recipe and just cooked whatever I could find in our house. He was often amazed by that. I loved watching him eat the food I cooked. His satisfied face and joyful eyes made me super happy. We often spent hours during dinner talking about our days, our thoughts, or just some silly stories.

But now, I have lost my best audience. The first four months after he passed away, I was living on carry-outs and leftovers again. If you have never lived alone, you will probably not understand that feeding yourself may be a challenge. When you are the only one eating, there's a greater tendency not to bother cooking because it feels like it just isn't worth it. Cooking for thirty to forty-five minutes, eating for thirty minutes and then cleaning up for fifteen minutes, that totals about one and a half hours! In that much time, I could write a blog post or reply to some emails.

That was my old way of thinking. Now, I am all into living in the present and making every day a joyful experience. Eating three healthy meals a day has become my top priority.

Cooking for others, for your loved ones, is pure joy. Cooking for yourself is where the true self-love begins.

Get Up, Dress Up, Never Give Up!

"No matter how I feel, I get up, dress up, and show up for life.
When I do, the day always serves up more than I could
have hoped for. Each day truly is a slice of heaven.
Some days the slices are just smaller than others."

- Regina Brett

August 25, 2017 (Day 210)

At the seven-month mark of my late husband's passing, I couldn't say it was getting easier, but certainly I was getting used to being a widow. Most of my days were kind of normal, but some days would not be so pretty. Those ups and downs were my new normal. I wanted the people who cared about me to understand that it was okay if I was down for a while; it was a part of this process. I always found a way to bounce back, and after each bounce back I would be even stronger.

"Get up, dress up, show up, and never give up" has been my motivation for a long time. It has been helping me hold myself together for many years.

Oddly, this summer break has been the most relaxing one for me. I set up a daily routine even before my break started and followed through every day. That meant I had an alarm every day, even though I didn't need to go to work. I cooked myself breakfast, lunch, and dinner. I went to the gym four or five times a week. Even on the most difficult days, I followed this routine. I believed, as long as I could get up, I had the chance and ability to make it a better day.

Dressing up for me was a no-brainer. It has been my own special way for years to fight back with all the difficulties in my life. It was like my fight song, to show all my troubles that I was still loving and taking care of myself. Most importantly, I was unbeatable. Bravery for me doesn't mean a person who never cries or has never gotten beaten up by life. It means no matter how many times and how badly beaten up they were, they can still stand up, even taller than before.

My man knew me better than I knew myself. Before Bob passed away, he said I would be fine because I had always been a fighter, I always rose after tough times. He asked me to continue enjoying my life without him. He wanted me to remember that I am worth it.

Yes! I am totally worth it.

I am not going to complain and say, "Why me?" I am not going to wait on others to rescue me. I deserve a happy life, and I was determined to get it. I am not going to give up on enjoying my life and chasing my dreams because I am a poor widow.

Everybody is worth it, and we should make this lifetime the best we can!

Keeping My Family Together

"When trouble comes, it's your family that supports you."

- Guy Lafleur

September 1, 2017 (Day 217)

I had a difficult decision to make many years ago after I learned that Bob was not able to have more children. I was hoping someday to have my own family. After some serious thinking, I decided to still marry my true love.

I went from being single to suddenly jumping into a wife and a stepmother role. My stepdaughter, Ashley, had already graduated from college, and my stepson was between his second and third year of college when Bob and I got married. I was quite scared, and I didn't know what to do when I was around them since I was only ten years older than my stepdaughter. Later, I figured out the only thing I could do was just simply be me.

After I moved to America, we lived in a hundred-year-old house that was in quite bad condition. We didn't have much furniture or decorations. We were pretty poor at that time, so Ashley took me yard sale shopping. I used my limited English to bargain and slowly built up quite a nice home. Now when I think back, I must have embarrassed Ashley because of my poor English and my hard bargaining.

I wish I'd had more time to spend with my stepson, Bobby, before he married. In the early days, he was in college, and we only saw each other a few times each year. Bob and I drove to his college every February for his birthday. It was not easy to visit often since it was almost a whole day's drive during the snowy season in Michigan. Bobby was quite distant with me, but I believed the only way it would work was to just be there for him. I was there for every important moment of his life since I arrived in America. He slowly accepted me.

Difficult times like losing a loved one can tear a family apart. Luckily for us, it brought us even closer than before. One weekend, we had a family gathering, and we all had a great time. My stepdaughter, my daughter-in-law, and I worked together, and we cooked a very yummy dinner. My future son-in-law was trimming the overgrown bushes in my yard, my stepson was helping in the garage, my two grand-dogs were running around, and my two adorable granddaughters were just being cute and happy.

Since my late husband passed away seven months ago, this was the first time that we all relaxed and enjoyed each other's company. As I looked around the dinner table, I couldn't help but think, *thank you so much for giving me a family!*

Trying to Be Positive

"Take responsibility of your own happiness,
never put it in other people's hands."
-Roy T. Bennett, The Light in the Heart

September 8, 2017 (Day 224)

Being positive became more difficult after I lost my man. Sometimes I would get angry and yell to nobody in particular, "What the heck? What did I do wrong that caused me to be punished like this?"

Life is not always fair. My mom never wanted me, and it still hurts to this day to think about this. Growing up struggling with food, clothes, and shelter made it so that I can never completely relax because I don't feel safe. My mom and dad had an arranged marriage, and they fought almost every day. My dad beat my mom, and my mom would run away, leaving my brother and me at home to clean up the broken dishes my dad had thrown and eating whatever food we could find. I hated my life and promised myself I would not live like that forever.

Yet, life, to an extent, is also totally fair. As adults, we live the life that is the result of many of the choices we have made. I moved to Shanghai a year after I graduated. I was so poor at the beginning—no job, no family or friends, and no money. But three years later, I was an HR manager and finally settled in that big city. I made a lot of good friends and later I met my husband.

Fast forward many years, I was married to my true love and finally built the life I had been dreaming of since I was very young— with a loving family and many joyful, happy moments.

In a lot of people's minds, I am such a poor lady. After many years of struggle, I finally had ten years of a peaceful life. Now that I've lost my husband, some people show pity because I don't have my own kids. They often ask, "What are you going to do now? Go back to China?"

A few days after Bob passed away, I called my family in China. This is what my mom said: "It doesn't matter how much you try; it is your fate. Now, you have become a widow even younger than me. You should have just accepted your fate and married a local guy as I wanted you to many years ago. Look at what you have done to yourself." Thanks mom! It seems like it was all my fault that I had become a widow and I don't really know how to resolve it!

All I know is that everything has two sides. I learned I had to choose to see the positive side. Those very difficult early days of my life did not just make me feel unsafe for my entire life, but they also taught me to work hard to get the life I want. My ill-functioning family didn't give me the love and support that every child deserves. Even as an adult, what my mom said about my widowhood is evidence that I still don't have that love and support from my family of origin; But this struggle made me treasure and appreciate kindness from anyone. Thus, I made so many life-long friends and have a very fortunate relationship with my American family, even after my husband passed away.

Ten years of a normal and peaceful life is too short. I deserve to have more, but it has also shown me what true love looks like, and it proved that even I, coming from an ill-functioning family, can still have a happy and healthy life after all.

Nobody is born to be a positive or negative person. We train ourselves to be who we are today. We are our choices. I choose to be positive and to be my best self that I can.

Love is in the Small Things

*"Enjoy the little things, for one day you may look
back and realize they were the big things."*
- Robert Breault

September 15, 2017 (Day 231)

Everyone who has ever known my late husband and I know how much we loved each other. Because of this, I often receive questions like, "How do you know if a man really loves you?" I am not a relationship expert, but I do believe love is in the small things.

Many years ago, we were quite poor, so we very rarely dined out. Because of our love of food, we often talked about the delicious foods we had tasted when we traveled around the world. One day, my man came home from work with a leftover box. He couldn't wait to show me what was inside. I opened it, risotto! One of my favorite foods! I had been craving it for a long time, ever since we had traveled to Italy. My man told me he had a meeting with some customers, and they took him to lunch. He was very happy when he saw the risotto on the menu. "Did you order two of them?" I knew he loved it very much, too. "No, but I had some, and here is yours."

Several years later, when my man took me to that same restaurant, I noticed how small the portion of the risotto was, and I suddenly realized that he might have only had one or two bites of the risotto that day. It turned out he only ate the side salad and saved the whole risotto for me. He said, "I love seeing you happy and enjoying your favorite food!"

When I was in middle school, my older brother once taught me to ride a motorcycle. I was doing quite well at the beginning, but when we were on the busy road, I panicked. My brother had to jump over to stop me from hitting someone. I didn't kill anyone, but after that I was quite afraid to operate any moving vehicles.

In 2008, I decided to get my teaching certificate, so I enrolled in a one-year evening program at our local university. At that time, I had just passed my driving test and got my license. Bob worked very far from our house. Every day he drove one hundred miles round trip to work. He knew how much I hated driving, so he went to work one hour earlier than usual just so he could get home a little early to drive me to my college. It was another two-hour roundtrip drive for him. When I was in the class, he went out to find some food and bring it back. On my break we would sit outside of the classroom and eat our dinner together. After that, he waited till my class ended, and then took me home. That was our routine once a week for the whole year. He was never late or complained about how much trouble I caused. He said, "I am very proud of you. You work so hard and I am very happy to be here with you."

My man often told me that he loved taking care of me. He said he felt good doing things for me. He never thought of all the things he did as if they were burdens, he took them as joys. He was not just good at saying how much he loved me; he was also good at showing his love by actions.

Love is all in the small things. Those small things can show how important you are to someone.

Finding Meaning and Hope to Live Alone

"Being alone and actually sitting with our own thoughts can lead to such growth and realizations that are rare in our everyday busy lives."

\- Kourtney Kardashian

September 22, 2017 (Day 238)

I was feeling very crappy due to a cold. It made it more difficult to stay upbeat, but I tried to fight back. My goal was always to keep my inner emotional and spiritual world calm and happy - no matter how the physical world changed around me.

It had been almost eight months since my man passed away. The first few months my goal was to survive. At that time, I was in shock. *What just happened? Is it real? Am I in a nightmare right now?* Then it came to a point where I realized, *I am totally alone and no matter how long I cry, how loud I yell, or how much I beg, he is not coming back.*

If I had a choice, I would love to have died before him so I wouldn't have to suffer the endless pain after he was gone. If I had a choice, I would grow older with him, with the only person who I truly felt was my soulmate. But the fact is that what I wished would happen was not an option I could choose. The only choice for me was to choose how to live alone.

My early years were quite difficult, so I know how bad a person's life can be. I have also been very fortunate to spend the last ten years with my man to live a normal but good life. After seeing both sides of life, and after going through both my dad and my husband passing away, I think I have found the meaning of my life. It is quite simple; just learn and practice to become the best of myself in this very short lifetime.

I was navigating through the first year of grieving. It was super hard, but I enjoyed victories every time I overcame some troubles or pushed myself out of my comfort zone to achieve a new level of self-confidence.

Living alone after being happily married for ten years was not easy. I constantly looked for Bob and talked to him. One time after my late evening meetings with parents at school, I reached for my phone to send a text to let him know that I was leaving. Of course, my hand just froze before I touched my phone because there was no one waiting for me. Those moments were usually very hard and often brought tears to my eyes. I'm slowly learning to become a complete person again who takes full responsibility for my own life and my own happiness.

My man taught me how to drive after I came to America. There is one thing that has always stuck in my mind about what he had taught me—I was very nervous about driving and often ran outside of the lines on the road. He said, "Look farther; don't always just look at what is close to you."

This trick sure helped me driving. I even find it is so true when it comes to dealing with life problems. When I am in my darkest times, I often tell myself, *don't just look at what is close to you. Look further - there is still hope.*

After all the storms, there will be rainbows, flowers, and all the beautiful dreams come true again. I don't know when exactly it will happen, but I know it will happen eventually.

No Longer Hiding

Behind the Rings

"The thought of being on my own really terrified me.
But then I realized being alone is really a cleansing thing."
- Lindsey Buckingham

September 29, 2017 (Day 245)

This past Monday marked eight months since my late husband passed away. I didn't cry like the previous seven months. I decided to just take it as a normal day. I had been under the weather for more than a week and that day I finally felt better and had more energy. On the way to work, I suddenly felt happy because I realized that I may have just pushed through a big step of grieving; I started to feel acceptance.

When we were dating many years ago, Bob was in America and I was in China. The longest time we didn't physically see each other was eight months. even though we did see each other on Skype every day for several hours. We celebrated his birthday, 4th of July, Labor Day, and Thanksgiving over the internet. Even with a twelve-hour time difference between us, we would eat together. The only difference was for me it was breakfast and for him it was dinner. These last eight months have been significantly more difficult than those eight months. There was no hope that he was coming back, and I couldn't see him on the internet. He was totally gone without a return date.

Over those eight months, I pushed myself outside of my comfort zone quite often in order to heal myself. First, I created a lot of new memories by traveling to Hawaii and Paris alone. There were no romantic stories from those trips. I made a few new friends after he passed away, it was new for me that they are just *my* friends, not *our* friends. Those experiences have helped me rediscover myself. I realized that I am very capable of conquering the world and being happy again without him.

By the six-month mark, I stopped wearing my wedding ring. It was a very weird feeling to be without the ring, and even now I still sometimes reach to that finger. It was a big change at that time, and I needed a piece of him to be with me, so I wore my engagement ring and his ring that I had given to him on my hands. Those two rings provided the safety net I needed at that time.

Then, by month eight, I decided to wear no rings because I realized that I should not hide behind those symbols. I am not married, not engaged, and I didn't need to wear them to show how much I missed him or how much I loved him. He was in my heart, and there will be a place for him forever that no one can replace.

It was kind of scary to be at the beginning again, but I know he will always be there for me. If I am sad or scared, I can still reach to him in my mind.

The real acceptance was not to always look for him, lean on him mentally, and ask him to give me signs or come to my dreams. I needed to count on myself to save my own day or make myself happy. It didn't mean that I was completely ready to move on. I still thought about him all the time. But I was finally eager to think about my own future.

It was still not clear what I wanted, but it was a big jump that I started to plan my future without him. I knew it would probably take a long time to come to complete acceptance, and I was nowhere near there, but taking off my wedding ring was a status change. It forced me to directly face this world, fail, cry, and then really learn how to be independent again.

Opening Up to a New Chapter in My Life

"You said this was only the beginning, I didn't realize that meant starting a new chapter without you as part of my story."

- Tannaz Sayadi, Write like no one is reading 2

October 6, 2017 (Day 252)

When two people really love each other, there will not be any topics that are untouchable. Before my late husband passed away, we had covered so many things that I needed his input and help with. One of them was about my love life in the future.

I still remember that day. We came back from the hospital, and his doctor had just given us a new estimate for how many days of his life were left. It was getting shorter and shorter after each chemo or radiation failed. We were holding hands and sitting in our usual spots on our conversation couch. I was crying, and he was trying to calm me down. I don't remember what exactly he said, but he made me laugh with tears in my eyes.

He always had the ability to make me laugh. I was looking at him and said, "You are a jerk! Where can I find a great husband like you again?"

He was smiling at me and said, "You are right. You probably will not find a guy like me. But you will find a different love."

Before my dad passed away, many years ago, he told my mom, "Don't marry again because you are my woman."

Before my man passed away, he told me, "I hope someone will love you as much as I did. You are the best wife, and you deserve to be happy."

What a difference! It felt so good that my man had given me permission to enjoy my life even after he was gone.

Although many people have asked me when I would start dating, I had never really thought about it until recently. My man was the only American guy I had ever dated, so I have no clue how to date in this country. In fact, I am very rusty about dating, period. I talked to a few friends about it, but I quickly ran away from this topic because talking about it was already making me sad. I told myself that I was content being single for now.

Yet, after hiding inside myself for a while, I realized that I wanted to love and be loved again. The pure love and happy marriage I had with my man were just too good to give up. But the idea of dating was very scary. I have heard so many horrible stories from my single friends about dating some weirdo or jerk. I also worried about my family becoming upset if they thought it was too early.

Luckily, I received blessings from a few family members and a lot of support from my friends and even fans. It was totally out of my control when I would meet another true love, or soulmate, again – three years, five years, or maybe the rest of my life. But I was not going to settle until I found the right one. I waited for thirty years to meet Bob; I am okay to wait again.

Most people may believe the chance of finding a soulmate twice in a lifetime was almost impossible. But I looked at it this way—I have seen what true love looks like, so I am more experienced to find it and build it again.

I was ready to open myself up to a new chapter of my life. It was scary but exciting at the same time. I had to be very careful, and I knew I might still get hurt. Either way, I was ready to come out of hiding.

FINDING GRACE

Finding a New Balance in Life

"Next to love, balance is the most important thing."
- John Wooden

October 20, 2017 (Day 266)

One of my students told me that she didn't like math class because she was not good at it. That spoke to me. There are a lot of times when we don't like something, not because it is not interesting but simply because we are not good at it. This sentiment totally corresponded with where I was regarding dating, both in person and online. I didn't go on an in-person date at that point, just simply tried online dating and quit.

I thought that since I had had a wonderful relationship with my late husband, I would know how to date. *It'll be super easy!* This theory was so not true! I didn't know how to flirt, especially online. I also didn't know how to play dating games. I felt horrible about myself after I read many articles about what not to do when starting to date online. So, I took a break until I learned more and felt more comfortable.

In part, I realized my grieving process was not done. I cried both on my way to and home from my father-in-law's ninety-fifth birthday party. My husband had been the youngest of four siblings. All of them called him the baby brother. He used to say that he had great genes in his family because everyone was quite healthy and lived a long life. This *great gene* was the last piece of hope we counted on after we found out he had a very rare type of cancer. Now everyone was there to celebrate Dad's ninety-five-year birthday, except for his youngest child.

That night, I went to meet a photographer friend for an upcoming photoshoot. He mentioned how much he wished he could do something to save his family member who was dying from cancer. My eyes instantly started watering. I was trying very hard not to cry--again, especially in public, but it made me realize again these moments might never stop. Something could just suddenly trigger those thoughts and make me sad when I least expected it.

I didn't mind being sad or tired, but I really didn't like the feeling of not being at peace. The dating tryout had brought out so many emotions and doubts for me. I was ready to find balance again.

Fixing Mistakes and

Adjusting Directions

"I felt bad for trying to live a happy, full life,
while my heart was buried in a dead man's chest."
- Kristen Hope Mazzola

October 27, 2017 (Day 273)

A few weeks ago, when I opened the door for dating, it didn't take much to see that I wasn't ready. My phone screen was still a photo of my late husband and me. I hadn't touched his closet at all. Nothing had changed in our house since he had passed away.

I thought I had been doing so well with grieving that I could push myself more quickly into the next stage and begin dating. I now know grieving needs a much longer time than I expected. It felt good to admit what I was able to do and what I was not able to do.

During that time, I experienced some horrible feelings about myself. I felt guilty and ashamed for all the time I thought about dating. I also felt I was not good enough to have the life I wanted. I was very confused about why it seemed so easy for my man to understand me, but in others' eyes I am needy and dramatic. After I finally admitted that I was rushing myself again, I felt better. I made a mistake and I was going to fix it.

I did a lot of self-reflection. The things I learned from rushing into trying to date were very valuable for me. This mistake made me rediscover myself. I was being too pushy, again. I also realized that there was no need to beat myself up for others' behavior or opinions.

About that time the song "According to You" came into my head quite often. It was a great song to teach me that if he is Mr. Right, all your flaws will be cute little charms — just like how I felt when I was with my man. I felt like I was perfect and wonderful the way that I am.

If a man couldn't make me feel at my best, that meant we didn't have the same values and standards. He would not be the right one for me. It had nothing to do with who was right or who was wrong. I am very picky about love, that's why I waited thirty years to marry Bob. So, this time, I would not force it to happen either. If it naturally happened, I would just let it happen. If not, I had so many important things to focus on—things like my blogging career, my fashion designer dreams, my fitness goals, and my plans to travel around the world.

After clearing my mind and picking myself up again, I was so much happier. I could see what was more important to me at this point and what I needed to do to make my dreams come true.

Dream Big and Believe in It

"Life is 10% what happens to us and 90% how we react to it."
- Dennis P. Kimbro

November 3, 2017 (Day 280)

It had been more than nine months since my husband had passed away. I had a super long week, so that Friday I cooked myself a nice dinner and decided to give myself a break by not turning on my computer. Instead, I watched a Chinese movie. It was just a typical chick flick that was based on a couple who met but, for whatever reasons, couldn't be together in three lifetimes. I had read some articles about reincarnation, and that evening I just kept thinking of my man. *Is he already starting his next life? Will he try to find me?* This life was still too long for me, and I really wanted to follow him to wherever he was. I cried non-stop for about an hour that evening.

I was comforted when I thought about ending my life and going to the next life to be with my man. It felt good and safe to know that he would be there for me. Later, I suddenly realized I had slipped into that black hole again, and I knew I needed to stop thinking like that immediately. That black hole of deep sorrow was taking over and controlling me. It made me bitter; I didn't care about anything. I needed to look away and look further into the future to see my hopes and dreams again.

Here's what I clung to: No matter where you're from, your dreams are valid. My life has totally proven this idea. If I didn't have some big and wild dreams when I was young, I could have been an unattractive middle-aged woman who had already totally given up on looking good or feeling good. I would probably have a minimum wage job and be living with an abusive husband with no skills, or ability to live on my own. I had seen many of my childhood friends in China who were living like this. It just made me feel so thankful for all the risks I have taken and all the wild dreams I have pursued.

Many people have said, "If your dreams don't scare you, then they're not big enough." Add me to that list. So, let's all take a few days to just dream big. *In the next ten years, where is the dream place that you would love to live? What would your dream house look like? What is your dream job or business? What type of people will you surround yourself with? Dream big and see those dreams as clearly and vividly as you can.* Write the answers out in great detail!

The only thing holding you back from a better and happier life is yourself. We can be our own worst enemies in so many ways, especially when we don't believe wholeheartedly in ourselves. We need to not just dream big but believe in it too! Hold tight to those dreams, knowing that we can and will do anything in our power to make them a reality. We need to have wild visions for our lives that we know we are destined to live, even if we are not living it today, in this very moment. In three years, you will start to see the change if you work for it. Remember, your current life is the result of your decisions that you made years ago. Dream big and make the right decisions.

I believe with all my heart that when I move out of a bad place in my life, I will be a better and stronger person. I have been tested, tutored and beat up, but I am still able to look darkness in the eye and tell it, "I will win!" Yes, life can seemingly suck at times. It can put you in a bubble of negative energy if you let it. You must break through the negativity and work toward building something new so that you can find the positive energy. Understand that all those tough situations are temporary.

Thanks for Raising Me Up

"If you look at what you have in life, you'll always have more. If you look at what you don't have in life, you'll never have enough."

\- Oprah Winfrey

November 17, 2017 (Day 294)

Right before Thanksgiving, I posted to my blog and thanked my readers. Here's what I wrote: "Thank you, to all of you who have raised me up during the darkest time of my life this year."

Expressing gratitude was important to me. Every night, before I fell asleep, I always liked to say thank you to God or whatever greater being was out there. I didn't have a religion, but I was still grateful to be alive and quite healthy. I know I was the person who could make my dreams come true, but God was the one who had the power to protect me from a drunk driver and all kinds of potential accidents. *Thank you for watching out for me!*

The most influential person in my life had to be my late husband. I had always been good at surviving because my anger motivated me to live. My man was the person who taught me how to love. I often asked him how I was supposed to live without him. He always said, "Life is beautiful. Enjoy it when you can."

He urged me to celebrate life even without the person I loved the most. Now I realized that there was nothing more powerful than the pure love of being alive, being able to breathe the fresh air, run under the sun, try delicious food and have great conversations with family or friends.

Man, I would not be the person I am today without you. Thank you so much for helping me grow from an ugly duckling into a strong and confident woman.

I was also super thankful to my family in America. They have given me a ton of love and support after my man passed away, especially my stepdaughter and her fiancé. They were at my house almost every single weekend to help me with my blog photos, proofread my posts, and work around my yard and the house. All of those jobs were taken care of by my late husband before, and now they were the ones doing it. One of my friends once said, "You don't have any blood relation to them and now that your husband has passed away, they are just your friends." But I would rather think they are my family. Friends can change, but family is forever.

I was also grateful for my amazing co-workers and great students. With their help and support, my daily working life was so much easier. Of course, I need to say how much I really appreciated all the friends I have made over the last three years on my blog and my social media. Most of us had not met in person yet, but I truly appreciated their positive comments that have lifted me up every day!

I was on my way to chasing my dreams and that was because all of them had raised me up!

The First Thanksgiving

Without My Man

"Every one of us is losing something precious to us. Lost opportunities, lost possibilities, feelings we can never get back again. That's part of what it means to be alive."
- Haruki Murakami, Kafka on the Shore

December 1, 2017 (Day 318)

With ten months of grieving, I learned one trick—create new memories. For the first Thanksgiving without Bob, I decided not to go to my brother-in-law's house like we had done almost every year. Instead, I planned to go with my friends to a Chinese buffet. I know, it sounds very sad, but I didn't mind this idea. I didn't want to ruin others' holiday because I couldn't help crying.

Then a great opportunity came up right before the holiday. I was invited to LA as Charming Charlie's Winter Ambassador. Both of my late husband's sisters lived near LA, so I decided to spend this first Thanksgiving with them. A friend told me my man probably knew I was struggling with the holiday, so he made this happen. I hoped he could use all his secret powers to help me through the holidays.

I had an amazing time working on the photo shoot and video filming for Charming Charlie. It made it very clear again how much I love doing this fashion gig. I was also quite fortunate to meet several amazing fashion bloggers in LA. I loved to listen to their stories and hang out with them. All the conversations were so heart-warming and enlightening.

My stepdaughter was quite relieved when she heard about this option and felt less guilty because they had planned to go to her fiancé's parents. I suggested we host our own family Thanksgiving at my house on the Saturday after I got back.

When the family Thanksgiving arrived, I was a little bit moody since it was the ten-month mark of my man passing away. Later in the day, with all the busy cooking and playing with my grandkids, the normal happy me came back again. My family requested that I cook some Chinese dumplings; they called them Thanksgiving dumplings (just like regular dumplings but on Thanksgiving!). I was all into creating new traditions and new memories.

The first Thanksgiving without my man turned out not to be bad as I thought.

Full-Time Blogging

"First you jump off the cliff and build your wings on the way down."

- Ray Bradbury

December 20, 2017 (Day 337)

On December 7, 2014, I had just started my blog "Color and Grace." I daydreamt every morning, while I was driving to my teaching job, that someday I would be able to do full-time blogging. Then, after six months, I ran all the numbers and set a goal for myself. The goal was after three years of blogging, I would be able to quit my full-time teaching job and do my blogging instead.

Thirteen days later than I originally planned, I finally did quit my teaching job, and began my first day of full-time blogging.

I should have let my school know this past summer that I would not come back, but I chickened out at the last second because now it was just me. I worried that no one was behind me telling me, "No worries, I got you." Yet, quickly after the new school year started, I realized that my fast-growing blog, and my full-time teaching job left me no time to eat or sleep. A few health issues arose, and I realized I had to make a choice.

I spent a few weeks researching, writing my business plan, and trying new things out to generate income for my blog. Soon after, I followed through with my business plan. I got more sponsors, and my life became even more crazy busy. At the end of October, my health issues became more and more serious. There was never a great time to quit a job, so I just "manned up" and got it done. I informed my school of my decision.

Luckily, I had a great school. They were sad that I was leaving but also very happy that I finally decided to pursue my dream. We all felt that we should keep the news that I was leaving a secret as long as we could so that my students would have a few more normal months.

Shortly before the end of the year, on a Friday, I announced to all my students, their parents, and the whole school that I was leaving. It was a very emotional day for all of us. Besides a lot of tears, there was so much laughter too. My middle school students planned to kidnap me so I would not leave them. One of my sweet sixth graders asked me, "Are you having a midlife crisis?" I had to laugh, not exactly, but it sure looked like it in a lot of people's eyes.

This year was for sure a special one on the record. I lost my husband in January and now in December I quit my job. The past eleven months had been the period that I rediscovered for myself who I am and who I wanted to be. I had finally come to the conclusion that I have the ability to make my dream become a reality.

This realization has totally changed the way I think and my entire life. There was confidence that I had never had before. So now all I needed to do was to dream, plan, and make it happen!

Embracing Changes and Creating My New Life

"Don't grieve. Anything you lose comes around in another form."

- Rumi

December 29, 2017 (Day 346)

The last few days at work were quite emotional for me, for my students, and my co-workers. I received many hugs, sweet gifts, and invitations to come back to my students' graduation ceremonies. Many of my students kept asking me, "Are you pulling a prank on us and at the last second you're going to tell us that it is just a joke?" It just broke my heart. There were so many kids crying on my shoulder and asking me to stay. I felt like I was a very cruel person to let them down. There were many kids who told me that I was their favorite teacher. The one who was always chill, caring, and kind.

Some of them told me that I had the best balance of nice and strict. Other kids I had never even taught came to me to tell me that they would miss me because I had had a very positive impact on them.

When the last class finished, and I was cleaning up my classroom, I left everything exactly the same for the new teacher and for my kids to feel this classroom was still their home. The only thing I took home was my school logo mug and all the letters and signs that my kids had made for me.

When I was tidying up the room for the last time, I suddenly felt sad. *This is real. This will not be my room anymore; I will not be here with my sweet students anymore.*

After millions of hugs and comforting many teary-eyed students, saying goodbye to my awesome co-workers, I was very emotionally drained. When I got home, I felt very blue. I had been waiting for this day for three years so that I could finally live in my dreams as a full-time blogger but saying goodbye to a beloved place and special people was very difficult for me.

After getting comfortable, I put on my headphones and turned on Pandora on my phone. I needed some music therapy, either to calm me down or let my emotions out. I knew I would feel better afterwards. Through the grieving practice, I came to understand myself more, and I've learned I need to give attention to the sadness, hurt, and other uncomfortable feelings, so later I would be more able (and likely) to feel the happiness and joy when it comes to me. I was singing along with some random songs and just let my tears run out freely.

Then, suddenly, a very familiar song started. "Somewhere over the Rainbow" was a favorite song for my man and me. This song has become a sign of Bob trying to comfort me many times since he passed away.

Listening to this song, I cried even more and wished he was there with me to comfort me and also to celebrate this moment as a big step toward me creating my life-long dream. Then I calmed down. Yes, he would be very happy and proud of me because this was one of his dying wishes too. He told me a few days before he passed away, "Never give up on your fashion dreams. You have it."

It may sound very weird, but I started to realize that losing my husband was not just a total disaster for me. It also has become a great opportunity for me to rediscover myself.

I had received so much love from many people. It was not the same type of love, but they all make me feel fulfilled and valued. Most importantly, I gained the greatest love from within myself. With this self-love and confidence, I was ready to embrace more changes and create my new life.

Pushing Through

Another Milestone

"Your grief path is yours alone, and no one else can walk it, and no one else can understand it."

- Terri Irwin

January 12, 2018 (Day 360)

I thought I was doing pretty well with my grieving journey. I had been very steady, happy, and calm. Until I started the process of cleaning out my late husband's stuff.

I liked to push through my emotions. It was fast approaching the one-year anniversary of Bob's death. I set my goal to move forward even more by removing him visually from my life. I had been relying on him too much. I smiled at his photos every day, talked to his ashes very often, and I held his stuff. Our house had been the same since he passed away. I figured it was time to push myself harder and jump up to achieve a higher level of grieving.

I started with our bedroom. In the beginning I was fine. Then, slowly, the sadness crept in. When I am blue, I like to put on my headphones and let music accompany me. I was going through drawer after drawer, the music was somehow all about lost love. My tears were all over my face, but I kept moving through. *I am strong. I can do it!* I kept telling myself.

When I took out his sleeping clothes from his nightstand, I cried so much I almost couldn't breathe. Then I saw myself in the mirror, unconsciously holding his sleeping clothing tightly to my chest. My goal was to clean up everything in order not to hold on to him, but I was heartbroken when I tried to put the sleeping clothes into the trash bag.

Then, suddenly, the music caught my attention; "Don't let me go, don't let me go." I was kneeling on the floor and wailing. In the end, I broke my rules and kept his sleeping clothes, also his eyeglasses. I was a fool for saying I was ready to move on. I was only partly ready. It was hard to admit my failure of judgment on where I was emotionally. But I was glad that I realized, admitted, and accepted where I was on this journey.

All I needed to do was adjust my goals and directions. Before this realization, I thought in 2018 I may establish a new relationship because I had been doing so well. I really needed to slow down.

For the most part, I was doing very well. But when it came to letting others into my life, I had some issues. I had to completely finish this grieving road all by myself.

There was no short cut. Dating would only interfere with the process and cause me more depression. I vowed to listen to my heart and keep pushing through. I was still planning to find my true love again someday. But I needed to give full closure to this one with my man first.

A Letter to My Late Husband on the One-Year Anniversary

"I know for certain that we never lose the people we love, even to death. They continue to participate in every act, thought and decision we make. Their love leaves an indelible imprint in our memories."

- Leo Buscaglia (professor and motivational speaker)

January 25, 2018 (Day 365)

Hi Man,

How are you? What does it feel like to live in heaven? Or have you already finished your reincarnation and are on the way to us? Please give me some signs so I can find you.

A few weeks ago, at a gathering event, someone asked me, "If you could have any superpowers, what would you like to have?"

I said, "To have the power to bring back my late husband."

It was suddenly deadly quiet. I know, I am still the same old party pooper.

One year ago today, you left us. There were some memories of the last few days of your life, they were just too painful to think about, so I set my goal to revisit them now. Wish me luck, Man.

We were sent to hospice a few days before you passed away. It was the most devastating moment of my life. There were no treatments, and no hopes left for us. Only death was awaiting. I was shocked, shaking, and angry. When we left your patient room, I couldn't help crying crazily. That hallway to hospice was the path to your death. Someone, or something, was really going to take you away from me, forever, no matter how much I begged. You were my best friend and my soulmate.

How could I live without you?

I was holding your hand and crying; you just smiled at me weakly and repeated, "I am so sorry. I am so, so sorry." I knew what you meant. You had said it a few times before that day. You felt so bad that you brought me here from China and now you would not be able to take care of me anymore. You often said I was cheated because we only had ten years together.

The night before you fully entered your coma stage, I was with you. You were rarely opening your eyes, speaking, or answering any questions. It was almost midnight, and I was ready to go to sleep too. I kissed you on your lips and said, "Good night!"

Your eyes didn't even open, but you answered, "Good night, baby!"

Then I said, "I love you," just like we always did before we go to sleep. But there was no answer. "Hey, I said I love you, Man!" I continued.

You opened your eyes and smiled at me. "I love you, too." And those were your final words.

Then, it was the last day. All of the family came, but you were already on your way and leaving us behind. Nurses came in and asked everyone to go to the waiting room so they could wash your body and change the sheets. I asked the nurse to give me a few minutes and asked the others to just leave us alone.

I was holding your hand and kissed you on your lips. Then I whispered into your ear, "Don't worry about me. I will take care of myself. If you need to leave, just leave. I am not mad at you, and I love you so, so much! You are the best husband, and I am very lucky that I married you!"

There was no response, but I noticed your breathing was slowing down. I was not sure at that moment if I saw it right. I stepped out and only a couple of minutes later the nurse called me in, and the doctor confirmed that you were gone.

I thought I was fully prepared for your death. But when that moment came, I just lost it. The only thing I said was, "Man, how could you do this do me?"

Sorry, Man, I should have been stronger and let you leave without any hesitation.

It has been a year since you left, and, yes, I am living without you. Just like you often said, "You are a very strong person, and you will be just fine." I wouldn't use fine to describe this first year without you, but I have followed through on my promise to you to take care of myself. I went to see a psychologist when I needed help. I eat, sleep well, and I am still following my fashion dreams as you wished. I even quit my teaching job and am now full-time blogging.

Before, it was always you who reminded me how much I have achieved when I doubted myself. Now, finally, I have learned to tell myself the same. You often said there was no regrets in your life because you have nice kids, loved what you did, traveled around the world, and married me.

Now I feel I could say the same someday when I die. I am not afraid of death anymore. If I die, I will see you and that is good news. If I live, I will live like I mean it and enjoy every moment. You see, there are no downsides for me.

Man, thank you so much for showing me what true love looks like and how to really live. You and our marriage have shaped me into who I am today. I notice your influence on the way I think and how I act. I see you in my heart, I hear you when I talk, and I smile when I think about you.

Goodbye, Man. Love you forever!

Making It Through the

First Year

"We are healed of a suffering only by experiencing it to the full."
- Marcel Proust (author and essayist)

January 26, 2018 (Day 366)

When I was young, the only family vacations we took were hiking and climbing mountains in my hometown. I used to hate it because one of the mountains had 999 stairs, and in many places, we had to twist our bodies like Spider-Man to get through it! It took pretty much the whole day to get to the top, and I was just so tired and grumpy. Then I remember, one day, I didn't keep looking up to see how far we still had to climb; I was only looking at the next three steps ahead of me and chatting with my family to kill time. Then, suddenly, I was at the top!

I didn't even realize I used the same strategy to deal with this life crisis last year until now when I look back.

January 28th last year was the Chinese New Year. We always celebrated it in the evening with a family feast. That was one of my man's favorite holidays. This was two nights after Bob was gone. My goal was just making sure we still had this dinner and that I didn't cry in front of the kids. If I did, I knew this family dinner would turn into a funeral. That was not what he wanted.

March 11th is my birthday. My man proposed on my birthday many years ago. He also gave me a very big surprise birthday party for my fortieth. I couldn't imagine how I could spend my birthday without him. But I had a very nice birthday because my stepdaughter and her fiancé gave me a very nice surprise day with several fun activities.

April 19th marks my ten-year anniversary of coming to America to marry Bob. We always went to a Mexican restaurant to celebrate. Now without him that day just didn't feel right. It turned out to be an amazing day because I went to work with Stacy London who used to be the co-host of the *What Not to Wear* show. After that, I had a nice dinner with my new blogger friend at the go-to Mexican restaurant that Bob and I enjoyed.

May 28th was my man's birthday. I was planning to give him a big surprise party, too, but I didn't get the chance. Somehow that day was more difficult than my own birthday. Our whole family went on a camping trip to honor him. We conquered another difficult day together.

June 18th was the day that Bob and I had met many years ago in Shanghai, and we chose the same day to get married ten years ago. This was probably the most difficult day of last year. But the first wedding anniversary without him actually became a very meaningful and fulfilling day. We hosted his life party a day after, as was his request. He didn't want a funeral; he wanted a party. I had to say, it was a great party with almost a hundred guests who shared great memories.

I struggled with the 25th of each month. It was a day I wish I could wipe off my calendar. When it hit September 25th, which was eight months after my man had passed away, I finally decided to take off my rings.

November 23rd was the first Thanksgiving without my man. I was struggling with those big family holidays. Normally we always go to my brother-in-law's house. But going by myself, was just too hard not to cry or not be sad there. Luckily, I had a distraction. About a week before Thanksgiving, I was sent to LA to shoot a campaign for Charming Charlies and create some new memories.

December 20th was officially my last day of being a teacher. It was quite scary and very emotional to finally decide to make that decision. On the 24th, we had our regular Christmas Eve family dinner. I was totally fine. But after the kids left on Christmas Day, I was a hot mess. Yes, the 25th of the month again! I cried for hours. This time, there was nothing to distract me and I tasted real depression.

January 7th, I started to go through my husband's clothes and all his stuff. It was a super difficult few weeks for everybody. But I am very glad that I pushed through again. I finally decided to remove all of his physical reminders to my heart and fully live my life in this new year. The 25th was approaching. I also set my goal to revisit the memories of the last few days of his life. It was not pretty. It took me quite a long time to finish because it was very painful to open the doors of those memories.

Then it was the 25th, this time it was the real one, the milestone one. I knew I would need some help. I was very lucky to be accompanied by a very dear friend. I just wanted to take it easy and be as normal as I could. She took me to get some new makeup, and we had very yummy Chinese food for dinner.

Now it has been more than a year, and I am more experienced about how to prepare myself for those difficult dates. I have been very lucky to have so many amazing family and friends who supported me along this journey. I wouldn't be here today without all the help.

2018, I am moving full speed forward to chase my dream and live my life as I mean it!

Back to China Alone

"Every single second is an opportunity to change your life, because in any moment you can change the way you feel."

\- Rhonda Byrne

March 2, 2018 (Day 404)

Last summer, many of my family and friends asked me to come back to China to visit. But I knew I wouldn't be able to handle the trip by myself emotionally. Bob and I met in Shanghai and there were so many memories to face.

Bob and I had a three-year, long-distance relationship due to his work assignment changes and having to wait on my visa to go to America. We talked on Skype every morning and evening for hours. There was a twelve- or thirteen-hour time difference between us depending on whether it was daylight savings time season. He also saved up all his vacation days and visited me every year on my birthday in March, sometimes on July 4th, Christmas, and the Chinese New Year when he could.

I was always so happy to pick him up at Pudong International Airport in Shanghai. But I hated the days when I saw him off. He tried very hard to put a smile on his face. He always walked quite slowly and kept turning back, looking at me, and waving to me. I was often very blue on the way home alone and stayed this way for a few days.

One year, while I was waiting for my man at the airport in Shanghai, I was a bit early. Suddenly I noticed a thirty-something-year-old Chinese man among many people walking out. He seemed like a successful businessperson. I noticed him because he was crying. That was very shocking for me because in Chinese culture, a man almost never cries, especially in public. I didn't know why, but I could feel his pain. I felt his loved one had passed away and he just missed the last chance to say goodbye. Maybe because it reminded me of many years ago when I ran into my house and found that my dad was already in the coffin.

I was hesitant about this trip to China alone. I knew I would be like that young man I saw years ago, shedding tears when I walked out of the airport by myself. My man was not there walking beside me anymore. On the flight to Shanghai, I was looking through the window and somehow felt my man was out there, above the clouds. Tears were running down my face, but I was also smiling. I knew Bob would be very happy to see me enjoying this trip, even just by myself.

I did enjoy it very much! It was probably the best visit since I had left many years ago. Probably because all the hard times I was going through, made me more grateful with everything and everyone! This twenty-two-day trip to China alone was a perfect testimony of my grieving progress. I didn't feel sorry for myself because of my loss. Instead, I enjoyed every single minute there and now I know that I could be happy by myself no matter where I am.

How We Met, Part-1

"You are a living magnet. What you attract into your life is in harmony with your dominant thoughts."

\- Brian Tracy

March 9, 2018 (Day 411)

"How did you guys meet?" It is probably the most frequent question I was asked regarding me and my late husband. I have to say; it was kind of unusual for us to meet. He was American and lived in Michigan; I am Chinese and lived in Shanghai. Physically it was almost impossible to meet. But then, on that very important day and time, our paths crossed.

I had run away from my hometown to this big and fancy city more than five years before. I changed my life dramatically, from almost homeless to co-owning a company with my best friend. There were a couple of short relationships, but nothing real. My heart just couldn't settle and was still looking for the true love as I had read about in books or seen in movies.

After I turned thirty years old, I suddenly was not in a hurry anymore. In Chinese society, it is like a life sentence if a woman hasn't married before age thirty. There is even a special word for women like me, *leftover women*. But, in fact, I was quite relaxed because no one gave me pressure anymore since they believed there was no hope of getting married at my age.

Without all the pressure, I spent more me-time reading and reflecting on what I really wanted. I came to the conclusion that I just wanted to be happy and enjoy my life whether I was married or not. Although society was putting a pity label on me, I found peace by just being the odd one out.

Reading fashion magazines, trying new skincare products, and learning how to take care of my body and my soul became my lifestyle. Seriously, I was at my best being a single woman.

It was June 18th in Shanghai, a very comfortable Friday afternoon. My partner, a female client, and I had a meeting at our office. We had a such great time that we decided to continue our conversation at one of my partner's favorite places, Paulaner Brauhaus, Shanghai at the Binjiang Branch. This was a German beer garden located in close proximity to the Lujiazui Financial District along the banks of the Huangpu River in Pudong. The restaurant boasts one of the most stunning views of Shanghai's historic Bund.

That very day, we sat at a table outside watching the boats going by, sipping German beer, and laughing at each other's jokes. Then, suddenly, a group of guys came to our table. There were two middle-aged Americans and one young Chinese. The young man asked us if they could share a table with us in Chinese. Just like all the beer gardens in Europe, customers need to share tables when it gets busy. So of course, we said okay.

The slim American man sat right next to me along with the young Chinese guy; the overweight American guy sat next to my client along with my partner facing me. At that time, I spoke almost no English. The only words I remembered from my college years were, "hello," "thank you," "how are you?" "I am fine," "goodbye," "yes," and "no."

I became nervous because I realized the American guys wanted to talk to us after we exchanged greetings. I had no clue what they said or how to respond and it was quite embarrassing.

How We Met, Part-2

"A soul mate is not found. A soul mate is recognized."

- Vironika Tugaleva

April 13, 2018 (Day 444)

My best friend and my client were translating for me during the conversation with these three guys. You know the instinct that every woman has that tells us if a guy is interested in us? The slim guy who sat right next to me was staring at me for a long time and making me very uncomfortable.

Suddenly, I felt someone's arm around my waist. My first reaction was to push the hand away from me. The hand turned out to belong to the slim American guy. I was not sure how to handle it. Was it just a common American gesture? Was I being super rude? Before I had the chance to think more, his hand was on my waist, again! I turned around and he was just giving me a big flirting smile.

I was very angry. *What is this? Who do you think I am?* No one would dare to do that in my own culture. I was being polite and now he was just given an inch and wanted a mile. I pushed his hand away again and stood up. I told my partner and my client I was leaving. They both left with me. On the way out, my partner told me, "You should see the look on his face!" I was like, *Do I really care?* I was already being very polite by not slapping him.

My partner joked a lot after this incident. She was the type of girl that most Chinese consider a beauty—tall, slim, pale skin with a beautiful face. Wherever we went, she was always the center of attention and there were many men wanting to talk to her. I was just a girl that no one ever noticed, but I was totally fine with it, and I was okay earning everything in my life by working hard. My friend even said one time, we could be best friends for many years because I was never jealous of her. Anyway, it was the only time that someone hit on me, not her. I seriously didn't take this American guy hitting on me as a compliment.

A few days later, my partner suddenly asked me, "Do you remember the other American guy with us last week?"

"Sort of. Why?"

"He wants to know your contact info."

All I could think was, *what is wrong with those American guys?* "No!" I answered.

She looked at me and said, "Do you want to learn English?" She always knew how to persuade me.

"Yup, I do, very much!" I felt embarrassed for not knowing English that day and I did want to learn more. "But what if the other American guy is also a jerk?"

"Just give him your email; he can't climb over the internet to harm you."

"Fine."

The other American guy and I started our pen pal journey. It took me at least two hours to write an email to him in English using a dictionary. He was always very patient with my painful grammar and confusing sentences. Oddly, Bob got me. He understood me very well. And I understood him. We had many deep conversations about life, and I realized I couldn't wait to receive his email every other day.

I still didn't think much about Bob because he was much older than me, he was not Chinese, and he was not the type of guy that I usually liked. But the more time I spent with him the more I realized underneath this overweight middle-aged American man was the soul I had been searching for and waiting for my whole life.

Finding My Life Purpose

"Grief can be the garden of compassion. If you keep your heart open through everything, your pain can become your greatest ally in your life's search for love and wisdom."

- Rumi

April 20, 2018 (Day 451)

On the eleven-year anniversary of starting my new life in America, I had been blue for about a week. There was some bad news from my family in China. One of my mom's sisters, who we are very close to, was dying. She was crying every day because she regretted that she had not enjoyed life for a single day and now she was running out of time. Then one of my dad's sisters died in a traffic accident. We saw each other quite often. She had even named me. But for some reason, no one really cared about her. The question: *what is the purpose of life?* followed me throughout the week.

I knew I needed to do something to make this special day not feel so heavy or painful anymore. I wanted to add some new hopeful meanings to this day, but I didn't know what or how. The only thing I knew was I needed to go back to my bubbly self somehow.

The way I cheered myself up had been listening to random motivational videos on YouTube. One morning, I encountered one of Oprah's old shows, and she was talking about the book and movie called *The Secret.* I started watching more and more about this topic on YouTube every day. And, finally, on this very special day of my life, April 19th, the anniversary of moving to America, I figured out my life purpose.

Bob was the first person who ever said that *I am beautiful.* His unconditional love opened the door of empowerment and helped me to see the real me, who is worthy, smart, hardworking, caring and *beautiful,* but he didn't complete me. *The journey of grieving has completed me.* I found peace with myself and with the world most of the time. But I still did not know what my life purpose was about.

I didn't have a religion, but I considered myself very spiritual. I had seen signs here and there in my life from the greater power above us, especially after my man passed away. But I still didn't know what God wanted me to do and why He had put me through all of these life crises. Then on this very special day, celebrating eleven years in America, I got my answer.

He put me through all the pain because he wants me to understand others' pain deeply. For example, when I am close to the 911 site in NYC, I just can't help tearing up. Now I know he sent my late husband to my life, to let me experience what unconditional love is, so I could learn and continue to give it to myself and others.

Then God took him away from me because He wanted me to discover the greater love, the love for myself, for others without any condition.

Now, I finally understand my life purpose: to give and to serve by just being the real me and telling my stories.

Start to Live,

Not Just Survive

"My mission in life is not merely to survive, but to thrive; and to do so with some passion, some compassion, some humor, and some style."

- Maya Angelou

April 27, 2018 (Day 458)

"If you were to die tomorrow, would you be happy with the life you lived? Would you be happy with the mark you left on the world? With the relationships you had? The last words you said to the people you love? Would you be happy with yourself?"

Those are some very powerful questions. Below are my answers.

Yes, I would be happy with the life I lived. I have made a lot of mistakes, and I have also achieved many things that I thought I was not capable of. There is no regret for me; my past has made me who I am today. Yes, I would be happy with the mark I left on the world. My mark is the big smile on my face. My mark is the big smile I put on others. Yes, I would be happy with the relationships I had. I had the best husband and still have the best stepfamily. I have many friends all over the world who adore me and support me. I even restored my relationship with my mom. I am totally at peace. Yes, the last words I said to my late husband before he went unconscious, were, "I love you," and he said, "I love you, too!" I don't know what my last words will be before I die, but I plan to never say anything hurtful to anyone. Yes, I am very happy with myself. I am glad that I have never given up and never let my dream die.

In fact, I am living in my dream life now! The definition of my dream life is very simple. It is just being able to sleep for eight hours and do the things I love every day, simply being happy, and enjoying every day I have in this lifetime. What does your dream life look like?

This past Wednesday has marked the fifteen-month anniversary of my late husband's passing. After all these ups and downs during this time, I finally have reached the point where I am no longer just surviving; I am actually living, living in my dream life! My dream is even getting bigger and bigger now because I have found my life purpose and I am going to make it happen.

My life purpose is to serve and to give by sharing my stories. Other than my blog and my social media, I also plan to write a book about my journey of *Living with Cancer* and *Life after Loss*. I am working on becoming a public speaker to share my stories on a different platform as well.

My final goal is to build a foundation to help all the people affected by losing a loved one. They will have a case manager who will follow them for five years. They can receive free grief consulting and job training to help them get back to their life again. I know, this is a super big goal and it requires millions of dollars to make it happen. But I'm doing it.

If your goals don't scare you, they aren't big enough, right?

Big Girls Do Cry

"Tears water our growth."

\- William Shakespeare

May 4, 2018 (Day 465)

I was never a cry baby. Instead, I had always been a tough cookie. After I married my soulmate, it had been so rare for me to even have a reason to shed tears. But during the two years since Bob passed away, I had set my own records of crying. The early period of dealing with my late husband's cancer diagnosis and treatments brought me to constant tears.

I remember the day after my late husband's first chemo treatment failed, and his doctor told us he had less than a year left. I held together very well and asked all the necessary questions. While Bob was getting his new chemo, I went to the cafeteria to find some food for myself. My best friend called while I was eating, and I told her the unfortunate news. She started to cry but I didn't join her. After I hung up the phone, I suddenly lost control. Hot tears unconsciously dropped on my plate while I was trying to eat. I put my head down on the table, but it didn't help. I just couldn't control the way I was feeling anymore. Suddenly, I felt someone tap on my shoulder. I looked up, to see a gentleman.

He asked me, "Are you okay?"

I wiped my tears and said, "Yes. I am okay."

He was so concerned and kept looking at me. I realized I needed to hide somewhere so I could express my heartfelt sadness without being a cause for people around me to worry. I ran into the bathroom, closed the door, and just let it all out.

Suddenly, I heard a lady's voice. "Are you okay, honey?"

I thought I was alone in the bathroom. "I am okay," I answered and already felt so much better after I had let all the tears out; my chest finally had room to breathe. After a few deep breaths, I stepped out to clean up my face.

A different lady suddenly said to me, "Tears cleanse the soul."

Throughout this *Living with Cancer* and *Life After Loss* journey, I slowly learned how important it was to take care of my emotions. If my tears suddenly come, it means I can't hold it anymore, just like the clouds can't hold the water and it becomes raindrops. I only let them out so I can have space to bring out newer and more beautiful smiles.

When I was told my youngest aunt had passed away, it didn't come as a surprise, but it made me very sad. We were very close. My emotion has always been a bit delayed in reacting to an event so I knew it could take two or three days before I had my release.

Sure enough, when all my step kids and their family were visiting, and I was cooking for them, I suddenly had to run to my room and cry for a short time. I missed my aunt and my late husband. I missed how it used to be the whole family here together, and it was so painful that it was not going to happen anymore.

Now I know being strong and crying are not in conflict. For me, being strong is knowing my limit and letting out the tears I can't hold. It is pushing the reset button so I will have the strength and positive attitude later.

Stepmom's Mother's Day

"Parenthood requires love, not DNA."

- Anonymous

May 8, 2018 (Day 469)

I never thought anyone would celebrate Mother's Day for me. My stepdaughter is only ten years younger than me, and I am thirteen years older than my stepson. I was never married before, nor was I a mother. At first, I didn't even know what to say or do with my stepkids. It was just too weird. Now when I look back, I felt sorry for my stepkids. They must have been super uncomfortable with me at first as well. Can you image your dad suddenly married to a much younger Chinese girl who looks like a teenager, can barely speak any English, and cooks weird Chinese dishes like chicken feet?

Ten years ago, when I had just married my man, I knew very little about American culture or in general how to be a mom. All I knew was I loved my husband so much, and that love extended to his kids. My ways of caring were very different due to cultural differences and it caused some hard times. Later, I figured it out: they would never call me "Mom" since they were pretty much already adults when I entered their lives. I shouldn't even think about whether they would love me back. I just needed be that special person there for them whenever they needed me.

In the second year after I moved to America, my stepdaughter lived with us for a while. We had some ups and downs while learning how to live together. One Friday evening, I was pulling weeds in my yard. Bob was back from work and came to me, saying, "You better clean up soon because we are going out to eat."

"Really?" I was very surprised. We were very tight on money at that time, and we hadn't gone out for a long time. Bob knew what I was thinking and told me that my stepdaughter was going to take us out for dinner. I was like, "Why?"

"I don't know, ask her when we meet her at the restaurant." He was being very mysterious.

During our dinner, my stepdaughter handed me a card and asked me to open it. I opened the envelope and pulled out a card that read, "Happy Mother's Day." I almost couldn't control my tears. I also got a pair of very cute earrings as my first Mother's Day gift.

The past fifteen months have been a true testimony for me and our family. Losing my late husband has brought us very close to each other, but the different ways and speeds of grieving almost tore us apart, too. Luckily, none of us gave up on each other, and now we are restoring our relationships again.

Being a stepmom, especially being a stepmom without my husband, I am super lucky and blessed to have my stepkids celebrate Mother's Day with me!

The New Normal

*"Grief is like the ocean; it comes on waves ebbing and flowing.
Sometimes the water is calm, and sometimes it is overwhelming. All
we can do is learn to swim."*

\- Vicki Harrison

May 18, 2018 (Day 479)

A few months ago, when I went to see my psychologist, I asked him a question: "When will I be normal again?"

He slowly answered, "Your life will never be the same. You will develop your new normal." I didn't fully understand what he meant until recently. I didn't even know my mood swings could be so dramatic. One minute I was laughing and feeling like life is so good, and then the next minute I was crying like a baby and didn't know what to do with myself. I didn't really like myself this way, but it seemed like I would stay that way for a while, maybe a long time.

I finally figured out my life purpose and came up with my plan to reach these humongous goals. Recently, I finally started developing my public speaking material as a part of the plan. Boy, I didn't realize going back through my whole life and looking at those memories could be so tough, especially those hard ones. I spent the entire day on my outlines for a PowerPoint. After it was all done, I was so drained and emotional. I could feel the mixed emotions in my chest, and I could barely handle it, so I went for a walk.

The birds were chirping, and so many trees were blossoming. The evening sunbeam was gently shining on my eyes, and I noticed that I had a big smile on my face. But, suddenly, the tears came too. I was trying very hard to hold them back until I reached a little wooded area. As I sat in the middle of the woods, the feelings of being unwanted, abandoned, and unloved by my mom when I was young came back to me again, and then the pain of losing my father and my husband.

After a while, I wiped my tears and walked back home. There was something beeping in my house. It was a smoke alarm in my kitchen on the tall ceiling. *Great, how am I going to climb that high to change the battery?* With beeping every sixty seconds, there was no way I could just leave it alone. *Fine!* I went to the garage and located the heavy-duty ladder that Bob used to love very much. I was trying to pick it up. Nope, it felt like it weighed more than me. I stuck my right shoulder under it and managed to drag it to my kitchen without damaging anything. Then another problem appeared. *How do I open it?* This fancy ladder looked so complicated, and I tried every way I could think of, but it just stood in the middle of my kitchen, not opening for me. This was my last straw. I sat on my floor and cried for about half an hour. If my man were here, I never would have needed to worry about these stupid things!

Indeed, it was a very small and stupid thing to have a mental breakdown about. But, that day, my emotions just took over and built up until I couldn't control it anymore. It was like a hurricane that just wiped away all of my confidence that I had developed in the past sixteen months. That day, I really tasted how powerful the native part of grief can be –– the anger, the pain, the hopelessness and depression.

After I calmed down, I asked my neighbor to show me how to open the ladder, and of course, it turned out to be super easy. I went to work in my yard for a few hours to relax after that, but that night I couldn't sleep at all. The next day, I worked in my yard for a few more hours. I was finally able to get some sleep that night.

There were more sleepless nights. I was surprised that I was hitting my rock bottom this late in the journey. I thought I was already way past the most difficult times of grieving. I really didn't want to hold on to this loss for this long. I wanted to be free and happy! I wanted to have a life without sudden tears and breakdowns. I wanted to have a life where I wasn't constantly sighing or fighting with my emotions. But I wasn't there yet! I was working on it.

What is the new normal for me? It is keeping smiling, even through tears.

How I Understand Death

at This Moment

"The mind is everything. What you think, you become."

- Buddha

May 25, 2018 (Day 486)

Death is never an easy topic to discuss. Since my husband passed away, my major battle going through this grieving process has been in trying to figure out how death, or losing him, can eventually make sense to me. In other words, I needed to make peace with his death and totally accept it.

Over the past two months, I have done a lot of soul searching by reading all kinds of articles, listening to speeches, or watching short videos about human souls. I had never given much thought to death and the soul before my man died. But, after all the learning and thinking, death was not such a mystery or scary anymore. I viewed it rather in a peaceful manner.

I believe the soul is a form of pure energy; it will neither die nor disappear. It just transfers between different forms. This human body is the vehicle of our soul for this lifetime. It begins with birth and ends with death, but in a bigger picture; it is just like a perennial, it comes back over and over.

When I thought about it this way, it made me feel better knowing my man had just left for a break, and he will be back to continue his journey. But the sad part is, when he does return, it would be in a different form. I wasn't sure if I would recognize him or if we would ever get a chance to encounter each other again. But, overall, I was very grateful that I shared this great love with him and learned so much from him too. His physical body was gone but his soul was living in mine, at least partially. I used to call that thing he had "stupid faith." He always said, "Everything will work out."

I was like, "Did you see the situation? Are you being realistic?"

I have now inherited his stupid faith.

The only power I have is to decide how I think or how I see it. I know I am not done with my grieving journey yet, but I feel I have figured out some of the most important answers at this moment. I am starting to feel my heart is not that heavy anymore.

How Traveling Alone

Has Helped Me

Through the Grieving

"There was something to be appreciated about grief. It wasn't just a sad place, but a strangely liberated place. In some ways, it made me reckless, but only in that it erased all the little fears I'd always clung to about venturing out into the world."

- Anonymous

June 1, 2018 (Day 493)

Everyone has their unique ways of handling things, including going through grieving. My special way of dealing with losing my late husband was traveling. In fact, the more accurate way to say it is traveling alone.

Traveling alone was one of my coping mechanisms. You might think someone is crazy to take a trip right after a loved one dies, but if the journey is individual and spiritual, what better place than the open road to dive right in?

Some of my deepest awakening moments of truth erupted in places that were not my home. When I stepped outside of my comfort zone, it was just me and me alone. I didn't know what I was doing at first, but that was one of the first steps in dealing with my grieving-- to confront and face and process.

My first solo trip started in March 2017, less than two months after my late husband passed away. My destination was Hawaii. You may remember reading about this trip, but I have never mentioned that I almost jumped into the ocean to escape my pain. Despite all of the troubles and emotions, on my third day in Hawaii there was a shift, an unlocking of some sort. For the first time since my man died, I felt a twinge of freedom. It was good to know that I still had the ability to enjoy life, even when I was alone.

I went on a helicopter without any doors in Hawaii. It was super windy, and I though many times that the little chopper could just lose control and I would die in the ocean. A tall couple from Australia sat behind me, and the wife was crying the whole trip because she was afraid. It turned out I didn't really care, and I enjoyed it very much.

My mindset was that the worst had already happened; there was nothing left to be afraid of. In the most thrilling way possible, none of it mattered anymore. I have never experienced this wild freedom before.

I went to Paris by myself in July 2017, that was about half year after I lost my man. It was my first international solo trip, and everything went very smoothly. I still remember that afternoon I sat outside of a bistro right next to the Louvre. It was a beautiful day; I was sipping my wine, tasting *foie gras*, and people watching. Suddenly, I felt complete peace come to my mind.

Surrounded by all the languages I didn't understand, my heart settled into a quietness that I had never experienced before. All the talking and noises faded and the only thing I saw was beautiful life unfolding right before my eyes. At that moment, I felt nothing but pure love and happiness! No sorrow, no anger, no confusion. My man was not even in my head. It was the first joyful moment without him.

Then a road trip to Canada, a flight to LA and Florida, and a whole month in China; after that was Houston, then London, Paris, Barcelona and NYC. There were more and more pure joyful memories I created without thinking of my man. These finally became my own trips.

Grieving is a lonely road and an isolating experience. But all the traveling has reminded me that there is a whole world out there still waiting on me to discover. My pain is so small. It is just a little drop of rain to the ocean.

Getting the Best Out

of Living Alone

"Without great solitude no serious work is possible."
- Pablo Picasso

June 8, 2018 (Day 500)

Last weekend, I went to our family dinner at my brother-in-law's home. On the way back, I purposely got lost.

Bob knew I liked scenic routes, so he was always very clever about which roads to pick. Besides, he seemed to have a built-in GPS in his head, and he knew just about every little back road everywhere. But not me, I am the typical bad driver who will instantly get lost without my GPS. Anyway, he used to take a very pretty route near Orchid Lake to show me the lakes and beautiful houses. So, my mission was to purposely ignore my GPS and try to find that route.

It felt pretty good that I was learning not to listen to directions, and it felt even better that such an uptight person like me could be this spontaneous. My thoughts at that moment were very simple, I had almost a full tank of gas and a few hours to spare, why not do something to make myself happy, right? I had no one waiting for me at home and no pets to feed.

I was alone, but I was not lonely. Well, at least 95% of the time I wasn't lonely. It had been wonderful living with my man. But I know it was just a habit. Given enough time, I could break it and recreate a new habit of living by myself. After sixteen months' practice, I was doing pretty well now.

These past few months had been the golden period of self-growth for me. Living alone gives me plenty of time to explore what makes me happy and what makes me sad. Recently, I had been training myself to be an observer of my own emotions because I have experienced more and more depressing thoughts, so I needed a new way to handle them. Since I was learning this new gig, I realized that I rarely fight with my emotions anymore; I neither ignored them nor let them take over. I just watched my emotions come and go, and I understand they are teaching me something. There was no need to be mad or panic. It would pass. In fact, there were a lot of times when I switched to observer mode, and those emotions just disappeared.

Before my man passed away, I thought living alone was impossible. Right after he was gone, I was eating and living for him to honor his wish. Then, slowly, I started to live for myself. Now I have come to enjoy living alone. I ordered some new outdoor furniture and planned to host several pool parties.

My goal is to grow even more and get myself ready for an even happier stage of my life. I will enjoy every day whether I am alone or with someone I love in the future. It is just simply because life is beautiful, and it deserves to be celebrated!

How Fitness Helped

Me Cope

"For me, fitness is not just about hitting the gym; it is also about an inner happiness and an overall well-being."
- Rakul Preet Singh

June 15, 2018 (Day 507)

After years of sitting in front of a computer, I had lost most of the strength of my body. It was so easy to feel tired, and I would get headaches often. I wasn't overweight, but I wasn't strong or very healthy either. When Bob was going through his chemo treatments, I was very stressed. My already troubled sleep was even worse. Sometimes I had two sleepless nights in a row, and I could feel my heart was working super hard in my chest. Soon after, I noticed my heart problems. Being aware of this sharp pain in my chest and having a hard time breathing made me feel lightheaded, like I had to hold on to something so as not to fall over.

I knew I had to do something to save myself. And the most important thing was to get in better shape to take care of my man.

So, I started to work out at home by using the *Beachbody* DVD. It's only a thirty-minute workout, but I was dying after my first two-minute warm-up. I had to cheat for a few sessions and pushed to finish the first day. When I stopped, I wanted to throw up. It wasn't pretty at all, and I was struggling. But I kept it going. Most days, my man was sitting on the chair across the room. He was already very weak because of the chemo, but he still wanted to keep me company. He would often fall asleep and then wake up from my workout music. He'd look at me and smile. There were a few times when I was crying during the workout because of the stress of my life. My tears would get all over my face and chest, but it somehow made me feel better.

After my man passed away, I found myself a gym nearby and decided to get my high school body back. That was the first step toward getting my life back. At that time, I didn't know that working out wasn't only about physical training. It has helped me so much with my mental health and dealing with depression.

I've been going to my gym for almost one year. Most of the months I wasn't traveling, I'd keep up a routine of going at least four times a week. Every day's class wasn't easy, but it was super fun. I started out with so many struggles, like before. There were seven stations, with each one lasting for forty-five seconds, and a total of four rounds. Before going to the gym, I never knew how much I could sweat! I'm very pleased to see that I can push through it day after day.

There were many days when I was angry and sad at my man's passing. But I didn't know who I should argue with or fight with. That invisible pain weighed me down all the time. Then my workout started to actually provide a visible target with measurable success. I treated every forty-five seconds of a station as the trouble and hard times that I was facing, and I fought through to win. Because of this, I gained control of my life back, forty-five seconds at a time. Through the journey of gaining physical strength, I actually gained mental confidence.

Knowing I can, and I am able, to push through anything in my way. That's success.

Celebrating Life with the Whole World

"I have found that if you love life, life will love you back."
- Arthur Rubinstein

June 29, 2018 (Day 521)

One reason I love traveling is to be close to nature, which often makes me realize how small my own pain is. It's just a drop of water in the ocean compared with the whole world. Last week, I went to San Francisco for a business trip, and I extended it into a mini vacation for myself. I visited Muir Woods National Monument and had the most magical and powerful experiences.

When I stepped on the tour bus, it was already quite full. There was an empty seat right behind the driver. I asked the lady who was to the left of the open seat if I could take it, and she said, "Yes, please!" We started talking on the way to the Muir Woods National Monument. When we stopped to have a quick peek at the Golden Gate Bridge, we were already feeling quite comfortable with each other. My new friend was working very hard to help me in photos.

She is a first-generation immigrant, like me, and she was on a business trip as well. We were both so impressed with the stories about the Muir Woods National Monument shared by the bus driver. When we arrived, we decided to continue hanging out together and took the hike together too.

I had never seen a tree so tall and wide in my entire life. The tallest tree in the monument stands at 258 feet tall, which is insane considering the seeds of these trees are roughly equal to the size of a tomato seed. The oldest tree is 1,200 years old (most are between 500 and 800 years old). As well as being tall, the trees at Muir Woods are exceptionally wide, reaching over fourteen feet. (You cannot get your arms all the way round one, they are too big!)

My new friend and I were like little kids so connected with the woods. We were both touched by the stories about the family circles from the sign we read: "Hundreds of years ago, a single large redwood grew here. Then disaster struck. The trunk of the large redwood died, perhaps by repeated and severe wildfires. In the photo here you can see the original tree trunk still standing upright, now a dead and blackened snag. Despite such terrible damage, the tree did not die. Below the ground, its massive root system was full of vitality. Before long, hundreds of young, bright green burl sprouts began to come up around the circle formed by the root crown of the original tree. Some of those sprouts have grown into the full-sized trees that today stand in a circle around the original trunk."

It's like life. I went through hard times in my life, from fighting hunger to family abuse and domestic violence, to losing my man. I have enough reasons to hate life, but the longing for life keeps me alive and makes me reborn over and over again. Like those thousand-year-old trees. They've been through everything. Yet, they're still there, calm and loving.

The night I came home, I received a message from my new friend. I was tearing up when I read it. "Hi, Grace! It's your friend from the Muir Woods forest. Just read some of your blogs. I'm sorry about your husband. Thank you for giving me perspective. You see, I've got cancer; almost three years ago, I had a surgery, then chemo. My hair grew back but not my eyebrows. But I gained a tremendous appreciation for life and meetings like ours. Your blog showed me how a family suffers when cancer hits one of its members. What can I do to ease their pain? Anyways, I'm going home tonight and will hug them warmly. And you, my random friend, be strong and know that you are not alone. Hugs."

Those trees and my new friend made me appreciate being alive so much again. There are no bigger reasons to celebrate life than just simply being alive! Always choose to face the sun. If it's cloudy, be your own sun.

From Widow to Single

"It's time to start living the life you've imagined."

- Henry James

July 6, 2018 (Day 528)

After more than sixty posts I have written in this *Life after Loss* series, I am going to end it today.

It started on February 6, 2017, which was about two weeks after my late husband passed away. Now, at a little less than eighteen months after his death, it is time for me to push myself to another level of recovery. From WIDOW to SINGLE.

Last week, I was at the salon, and the new hairdresser asked me, "Are you married, with kids?"

I was a little hesitant and said, "I am a widow with two adult stepkids."

Of course, she said, "Oh, I am so sorry."

It was never my intention to make others feel sorry for me because I haven't felt sorry for myself for a long time. I know it is time to take off the *widow* label.

I was quite emotional when I started typing this title. Writing about my *Life After Loss* journey, with many making their way into this book, has been my way of coping and my way of grieving. Every single word was from the bottom of my heart. Real and raw. With tears, with struggles, and with the happiness of awakening. I never had the intention of writing them for others. They were for me to document my journey, but because of those posts I have received thousands of emails, messages, and comments from strangers. They all said the same thing: my posts have helped them, or someone in their life, to see hope again.

Now that this *Life After Loss* series had ended, what is next? I plan to start a new series about self-empowerment which will be called *Being the Best of Me*. This topic has been very dear to my heart since my husband passed away. I used to doubt myself all the time, and he was the one always helping me to find my confidence. But now I am confident - no matter what the circumstances are - because I finally know who I am and what I am capable of accomplishing. Self-empowerment is about practicing giving unconditional love to ourselves and growing into the best version of ourselves.

I have waited for this moment a long while. It is quite exciting and a bit scary because I had gotten used to carrying around my widow label and hiding behind it. Now I am a single woman. I cannot wait to see what I can create with my life.

PART FOUR

Being the Best of Me

(2018–2019)

Seeing the Brutal

Truth of Myself

"You are imperfect, you are wired for struggle, but you are worthy of love and belonging."

- Brene Brown

July 13, 2018 (Day 534)

I have struggled my entire life to believe that I am enough. To believe I am good enough, smart enough, brave enough or beautiful enough. Childhood damage has been far stronger than I could imagine. I thought this past year I had made huge progress on self-empowerment and making peace with the past. I didn't know that I still have so many emotions.

Since my intention is to share my stories with more people, and encourage others to give their dream a chance, I had to go back to where I was to take my audience to where I am now. Since day one, I started going back to those memories. I felt angry, shamed, helpless, and confused. It made me realize that those emotions are still there. My surface emotions were cleaned up, but there was still a lot to deal with underneath.

I presented a PowerPoint to my mentor and another friend a few days ago. While telling my stories, I was uncomfortable. Somehow, I felt shame. I felt horrible thoughts of not being good enough, so my mom did not want me. That is the same reason my ex-boyfriend abused me. Of course, I know that was not the truth, but I had a hard time removing those thoughts from my head at that moment. When my mentor and my friend gave me feedback, I couldn't help but feel offended. I was a paid public speaker while in China and quite proud of what I had achieved. But when I received the feedback, I felt not good enough, again.

I tried controlling my emotions. No matter how much I tried, my intense body language and facial expressions still sold me out. I was quite shocked at myself, too. After all the hardships that I had been through, what could make me feel self-doubt again? But, as it turned out, I still couldn't take any criticism. Now I understand why I always work so hard and often became an overachiever. It was because I thought, this way, people will give me less criticism. Now I can see how underneath this overachiever is a person still hurting from childhood damages - a person struggling with their identity and self-worth.

It was good to see the brutal facts about myself. I struggled with my emotions, trying to hold it together and get the task at hand done. It was not pretty at all, feeling torn apart by all the criticism. I was actually getting torn apart by my insecurity. My mentor and my friend were very nice to me, but all I could feel at that moment was the shame - a feeling of not being good enough. Then I was feeling bad about making such a scene while they were trying to help me out.

At this moment, I am glad that I saw this brutal truth about myself. Also, I understand that I have a long way to go to reach full recovery from my childhood damage. Without fixing it, or accepting it, my confidence will only be on the surface level.

Beautiful Inside and Out

"Outer beauty captures the eyes. Inner beauty captures the heart."

- Anonymous

July 20, 2018 (Day 541)

I have never felt truly beautiful until this year. This is the year when my inner beauty and outer beauty have finally matched. Every time when I say "I am not that beautiful," it is quite interesting to see the look on people's faces. They are kind of like, "Are you kidding?" No, I am not kidding or trying too hard to come off as humble. My family was super poor, and my mom never wanted me. All my clothes were hand-me-downs from my older brother. I had pretty much zero knowledge about how to look good when I was young. My mom had very limited style advice. So, I was never exposed to fashion or beauty until I moved to Shanghai in my late twenties.

I always knew I had inner beauty, but I felt my appearance did not match. My best friend when I was in Shanghai was a very beautiful girl. Guys were fighting with each other to talk to her. I was the invisible one next to her. It did not bug me at all. Because she had her way to get what she wanted, but I have always believed that the best way to earn the life I wanted was through hardworking.

Bob was the first person to ever say I was beautiful. Of course, I didn't believe him. For my whole life, I received compliments saying I was smart, hardworking, or nice. But *beautiful* was foreign to me. I did not believe I was beautiful (or ugly). I felt I was a very normal, average-looking girl who blended in.

My man would say, "You are beautiful," day after day, and year after year. I told myself: *This guy has such faith in me. I better not let him down. I can get my college degree, manage more than 100 people in a department, and run my business. I can find a way to make myself look and feel beautiful and let my inner beauty shine through.* So, I started reading all kinds of fashion magazines. and watching YouTube videos to learn how to apply makeup and do simple hairstyles. I also learned how to dress tastefully. After a few years, there were more and more people starting to compliment my style. All the nice feedback from strangers had given me the confidence to start my fashion blog.

Yet, I still did not believe in my beauty after four years into blogging. Even though I was receiving a lot of compliments about my beauty. That is when I realized applying makeup, curling hair, or putting together a cute outfit are easy tasks to learn. But true confidence is hard to reach. My outer beauty has grown since I started my blog. And now, finally, my inner beauty started to match up with the feelings of my outer beauty these past two years. Since I switched my attention to self-growth and self-empowerment, I love who I am and how I look. I love getting all dressed up to go to an event. I also love working in my yard without makeup and fancy clothes. I know I can look good. But I also know that my warm smile and contagious laugh are more beautiful than any of my designer handbags.

Being beautiful inside and out is balancing inner growth and outer growth. I like to see my love of life shine through my appearance. My style and fashion help me to speak about my inner world. Looking and feeling beautiful has nothing to do with what others think. It is all about being comfortable in my own skin: a picture-perfect look to please my own eyes or rocking a bare face while doing yoga to please my heart. Either way, I am feeling beautiful. Because I am on my way to being the best of myself.

Setting a Peace Treaty with My Childhood Abuse

"Everything we hear is an opinion, not a fact. Everything we see is a perspective, not the truth."

\- Marcus Aurelius

July 27, 2018 (Day 548)

Everybody is damaged, on a unique level. And everybody has holes in their heart. Most of the damage or pain was from our parents when we were little, intentionally, or unintentionally. The results are the same; we often feel insecure, or not good enough.

As long as I have had memories, I remember my mom being the one who made me suffer the most. Now when I look back, all the physical punishments were not that powerful. I do remember I was very scared of her. But her words, or the attitude of disliking me, hold a longer impact on me. She and her siblings would often laugh at my looks, especially my big nose. She would say, and this is a direct quote, "It is so ugly. Just like her dad and his family." My older brother has the exact nose but somehow, in her eyes, he was so cute and lovable. So, he got everything, and I got his leftovers or hand-me-downs. My older brother used to like singing, so he was the star. I once tried humming along, and my mom said, "Your voice is like a man's. No one wants to listen." Her constant criticism and putting me down made me feel terrible about myself. It made me double my efforts to please her. But, her look of approval was never given to me. All her love went to my older brother.

After my man passed away, I decided to end my suffering. None of my family has ever visited me from China. No one was at my wedding nor by my side when my husband passed away. Ten years of living in America, and my mom had never called me once. It's always been me calling her. This past February, I decided to give it one last try at resolving our relationship. So, I went back to China to spend some time with her. It wasn't easy at first, because I didn't feel comfortable with my mother. We've never been close, and I ran away from her right after I graduated from middle school. I lived in a dorm for my entire high school and college years. After college, I moved out completely. So, I didn't really know her that well. All the memories that I have are of how terrible she was when I was young.

A friend of mine has a very similar mom. At some points, her mother was even worse than my mother. We used to tell each other how horrible our mothers were, and cry together when we were young. Last year when I was in China, I was very surprised to hear her say, "I am very grateful for everything, even my mom." I asked *why* and *how* she could feel that way. She looked at me and said, very peacefully, "I understand her better now. She didn't know the best way to love me, but she tried her best." That's the moment I started to wonder if I'd been too stubborn to see another side of the truth. Which is: I know I need to forgive my mom because that's the only way I'll set myself free. The problem was I didn't know how to not feel angry with all she has done to me.

My mom finally said "sorry" after many conversations this February. I'm not entirely clear if she meant it. But the time when I was with her, I was the center of her day. This treatment was very strange to me, yet I loved it. That's when I began to realize that I didn't really know her. She had softened so much, compared to when she was younger. She constantly wanted my attention and my love. I was quite confused.

After I went back to America, she bought a smartphone and learned how to use video calling. She even learned how to type so she could leave a comment on my post on WeChat (the Chinese version of social media). Then we began talking once or twice a month for about one hour each time. Our recent conversation got me thinking that I finally have the peace I've longed for.

When I picked up her video call, and saw her face with a huge smile, I knew she was super happy to see me. I felt the happiness through the screen. She told me some stories of the early years of her life, and I had to hold my tears back from feeling so sad for her. I had to fight so hard to get my life today, but I forgot she had to fight ten times harder than me to simply survive. Then she mentioned that my older brother never had a toy when he was a kid. Something became clear in my mind. I'd held a grudge for years, but I forgot that I wasn't the only one suffering the effects of being poor. I often told others that I never had a toy, but my older brother never had one either. I never heard him complaining at all. At the end of our conversation, I asked my mom if she remembered the things she had done to me. She was thinking very hard and she said, "Not really." I could read her face, and I knew she wasn't lying.

Clearly, we didn't have the same memory. She thought she tried her best, and I was hurting so badly for my whole life because of her. I don't have a time machine to fly back and see what exactly happened. I'll never know if she was that evil mom, or if I only saw what I chose to see. Now, I only know how she has changed a lot and become a pretty good mom. I decided to set a peace treaty with my childhood abuse. I can't change the past, but I love to enjoy the present moment with her. I also can't wait to create more happy memories with her in the future.

Finding the Truth of

Loneliness

*"The best friend you will ever find is you. You must love yourself
with joy to fill your heart with bliss and happiness."*
- Debasish Mridha

August 3, 2018 (Day 555)

A few nights ago, I was on my way home from an event. I followed my car's GPS, but it was not updated so it didn't know anything about the freeway closure. I ended up in Detroit, somewhere in the dark of night. It made me a little nervous to stop at a gas station and fire up my Google Maps app on my phone. Finally, I was on the right freeway.

It was quite late, and I was very tired. Suddenly, I heard some huge engine roaring right behind me. Before I reacted, I saw the car near me almost tip over. It was trying to avoid getting hit by the Dodge Challenger between us. There was not even a lane between us! The Dodge Challenger just pushed that car to the side of the road and cut in front of me, then gone! I was like, *What the heck?!* Then a second Dodge Challenger did the same thing on my left, and a third came in front of me from my right. It was like a car chasing scene in Hollywood movies. Luckily, there were no car crashes.

I suddenly wanted to tell this to someone, just like the day I almost drowned in my pool, or just like the day I signed the biggest contract with a sponsor. But I did not have someone whom I felt comfortable to text or call late at night. There was only one person that I know who always loved to hear from me. No matter how late, no matter how busy he was, and what country he was in. That person was my man. At that moment, I felt lonely.

Being alone is not the cause of loneliness. I remember being younger and feeling lonely in the most crowded places. I have felt total loneliness when in some not-so-good relationships, too. Feeling lonely has nothing to do with whether I'm with someone, or if I have a lot of friends. Feeling lonely is lacking connection.

Recently, I figured out that the connection is not with someone or something. It's with myself. When I hang out with someone who really understands me, adores me, and knows how to make me laugh, my level of loneliness is totally reduced. But there is no one, not even my soulmate, who can cure it. If loneliness is depending on others, then I have a 50% chance of getting disappointed. I can't control what others do. I can't make him or her think just like me. When their values or behaviors aren't aligned with mine, I'll feel like I'm not being understood, cared for, or loved. And I'll feel lonely.

The only one I can truly control is me. The truth of loneliness is the lack of connection with myself, with my soul. I love learning about myself, discovering something new about myself, and sometimes I'm amazed by myself too.

I'm going to be my own best friend first and enjoy the inner conversation with myself. I'm not going to depend on others to love me, support me, or forgive me. Because someday when they stop, I'll be sad and lonely. I'll give myself unconditional love, treat every inhale as a new beginning, and every exhale as letting go. Life can take everything from me, just like it took away my late husband. But it can't take my mind away. Change my mindset, change my life!

Focus on What I Want

"The law of attraction states that whatever you focus on, think about, read about, and talk about intensely, you're going to attract more of into your life."

- Jack Canfield

November 16, 2018 (Day 660)

Everybody knows we need to focus on what we want. But the reality is we often focus on what we DON'T want.

Last week, I was invited to an event in a nearby city in Michigan. I was chatting with a friend the night before my trip when I said something like, "Let's see how long it will take me to get there since I always get lost." My friend pointed out to me "Be positive!" I suddenly realized that my energy was focused exactly on what I didn't want!!

Why am I doing this?! Later on, I found my answer. The fears of driving the long distance and in the unfamiliar area had me worried. Then I realized that over the years, I had built a habit, of the mindset *if I worry, I'll never have a bad surprise.* But the truth is, when I am always concerned, and on edge, my nervous system is on high alert. Mental tension translates into physical tension, that is why I often notice my sore neck and super tight shoulders. That physical stress made me feel like I should worry because I was feeling so physically agitated. What a strange cycle!

After I cleared my mind and intentionally focused on what I wanted, which was to have a smooth road trip, everything turned out perfectly fine! I used my car's GPS and also set my phone GPS just in case there were any surprise constructions on the way. Then I popped in the motivation CD and listened all the way there.

The event was very successful, and I had a great time. When I got back to my hotel room, I was exhausted. Before bed, I checked the weather, and I was worried again. Winter Weather Advisory! It predicted three inches of snow the next day. My little car didn't do well on the snowy roads, and my snow tire appointment was the week after. When I was laying in the dark, I saw myself in the ditch and standing in the cold. I felt my breathing get heavier and my heartbeat getting faster. I suddenly realized that I did it again! I put all the scary images into my own head and made my body suffer just by imagining. So, I asked myself *What do I want now?* The answer was very clear, and that was that I wanted to be able to sleep at this moment. And so, I did.

The next morning, the first thing I did after I was up, was open the curtain to check. The weather forecast was correct! I texted my stepdaughter, and it was snowing at home as well. So, I focused on what I wanted, which was a safe and smooth trip home. I switched around my calendar and waited a few extra hours until the snow was slowing down and then headed home. It turned out the freeway was not bad at all. In fact, the trees and fields were so beautiful with a fresh coat of snow.

When I truly focus on what I want, my life is clearer, easier and I feel less worried.

Improving My Emotional Fitness

"I am determined to lose my stubborn emotional belly fat!"

- Grace Liang

November 30, 2018 (Day 674)

Physical fitness is easy to see from the mirror, or a scale. But emotional fitness is quite hard to see so it makes it difficult to manage. I thought I had done so much work on myself in the past two years and I thought I had gotten pretty good at understanding and managing my emotions. But the holidays bring so many mixed emotions and I was surprised by how emotional I was, again!

I hosted our annual family Thanksgiving dinner at my house. We had great food as usual, and I had a great time hanging out with my stepkids, especially my two adorable granddaughters. After everybody left that night, I suddenly felt so lonely. I hadn't had this feeling for many months. Then my friend called me. During the conversation, somehow, I was hoping this friend could save me from the horrible loneliness I was feeling at that moment. Since we are quite close, I thought this person should not just understand me, but also should take care of me by fulfilling my neediness. However, this friend was quite confused and frustrated with not knowing what to do.

It took me about two days to finally understand myself and re-center my emotions. This event was a great opportunity for me to notice that maybe I had gotten my physical body back through almost two years of gym routines and healthy eating - but my emotional fitness level was still low. Improving my emotional fitness became my focus.

The first question that came to my head was, *how do I improve?* I didn't really know at first, then when I was in my gym class, I figured it out. To improve my emotional fitness just like the physical fitness, I needed to know where I was first and then set a goal with what I would like to achieve in three months, half a year, and one year. I have pretty clear self-awareness for the most part, but for certain areas, I have to just put more effort to figure it out so I could get the inner peace that I always wanted. Those emotional areas were like the stubborn tummy fat. I knew it would take a lot of work to see the results.

Then the second question was, *what is the action to reach my emotional fitness goals?* The most effective way for me was to step out of my emotions for a while. It sounds weird, but I have learned that I must pause my feelings, then step out to watch it like a movie, or a play. We often become very clear when we listen to another person's story but struggle when we are *in* the story. So, I observed my story like another's story, and this way I could understand my situation better.

I also tried a new approach after I have learned the golden rule of *focus on what I want.* Basically, if I focus on the problem, all my brain can see, and my body can feel is this problem. Eventually, this problem became the major thing of my day and my life.

For example, I lost my late husband. It was a huge problem. I could focus on *Why did this happen to me? What I have done wrong to get punished so badly? Why I am always having bad luck?* Obviously, this focus will result in me being angry, suffering in more pain and depressed.

But when I shifted my focus on other things, like my fashion dream, I started to feel the joy of life again and it helped me to rebuild my confidence and emotional strength. Temporarily not thinking about the problem that I lost my late husband, helped me gain the power to revisit the problem again with a better level of emotional fitness. I was so used to focusing on the problem because I wanted to find out why and how to solve it. It only made the problem bigger, and I suffered even more.

It is just like physical fitness; emotional fitness takes a lot of effort to work on daily by observing, reflecting, letting go for a while, learning different ways to handle situations, and eventually to gain a more powerful mindset that can turn everything into a possibility and make the best out of everything that happens in life.

Practice, practice and practice, I am determined to lose my stubborn emotional belly fat!

How Would You Direct the Movie of Your Life?

"My movie will be a combination of adventure, family, romance, comedy and very little drama!"

\- Grace Liang

December 14, 2018 (Day 688)

During the holiday seasons, I like to watch movies to build up my holiday cheer. A few nights ago, I watched *The Christmas Chronicles* and really loved it. I am not from a long family line of true believers, but I really believe in the miracle of life. I think Santa represents the miracle power that we all have in us, and we just have to choose to believe in ourselves.

This movie got me thinking, what if I am the director of this movie called *My Own Life?* What type of movie am I going to make? Drama? Action? Adventure? Comedy? Crime? Family? Fantasy? Mystery? Romance? There are so many choices!

In fact, *I am* already the movie director of my own forty-four years of life. If I watch my own life movie as a stranger on Netflix, I have to say it is quite an interesting one. At least to me! It has a very humble beginning. I struggled with survival, love, loss, finding life purpose, and then living life fully. My movie shows me as a human being at my best, my worst, and everything in-between. But eventually I made it to a happy ending.

Based on the average life expectancy, I probably still have at least another forty years of life to continue in this movie called *Grace's Life Story*. How would I direct the movie about my life intentionally? It sounds like I need a vision board and life plan before writing this script for my movie, right? In fact, I do have a vision board for 2018 and plan to update it soon before the New Year, 2019. I usually block one day to write down a super detailed life plan, too.

Anyway, according to where I am at now in my life story, I determined to create more happy ending stories. I know there is no way to be happy all the way to the end, but at least, I know how this life thing works. It's not the life event that decides my quality of life; it is what I think or do with those life events. For example, I lost my husband, and this event interrupted the quality of my life, but after I survived, I created a new way to be happy again. The new way is to take the life after the loss as an opportunity to rediscover myself and create a new way of living without him.

The quality of life starts with how I communicate with myself or choose to believe. For example, a few days ago a friend said that he thinks I am a successful person. I answered, "No, I don't think so." I am still so far, far away from making the million dollars that I want to start my Life After Loss Foundation. I could only barely support myself. Later when I chatted with a different friend, he corrected me "You *are* successful! You have overcome many times and turned your life around. You are doing what you love and are happy most of the times. Being successful is not just about money."

That is so true! How can I fall back to that old habit again?! I instantly felt different. *Yes, I am successful!* Those moments of realization just showed again that we determine how we feel by the meaning we give to the event, or whatever is happening in our life. Now I know this secret: I can decide what meanings to give everything in my life. Damaged childhood? Nah! It was just hardships that I encountered, and I can heal myself by learning how to love myself and forgive others. Life is unfair and I am depressed because I lost my father and late husband? No, it was just the push to make me truly independent and to pursue a higher level of self-awareness without attaching myself to anyone. I am out of luck finding my soulmate again since I already had one before? Naah! I am very experienced on how to create a close relationship so when I see it, I can recognize it.

What will my life movie be about in the next forty or more years? I am determined it will be about passion and love for life. My movie will be a combination of adventure, family, romance, comedy and very little drama! What kind of movie will you direct your life to be?

From Survive to Thrive

"Life is not happening to you; it's happening for you."
- Tony Robbins

January 25, 2019 (Day 730)

This is the day I would love to skip or forget forever. It is the date that my beloved husband passed away two years ago.

That day was the day my wonderful life completely shattered. I didn't want to do anything but hide and cry to death. But I couldn't. My man asked me to live, for him! Everything that felt important before felt meaningless without him. I wished could trade in my whole world to take him back! The only person I wanted was him!

I really had no idea how to live without him. The only thing I knew, as I had promised my man that I will take care of myself and our family. At that point, it was just one breath, one meal, one day at a time —surviving. That was the only way I knew how to honor his love.

During the first year, I slowly noticed that I could still be happy again, even by myself! Like a little kid learning to walk, I started to push my limit and tried to live for myself, not just for him. I had learned so much about myself in the second year and also gained so much confidence. The fact is, I am still very capable to chase my dream life alone, without him, or anyone else. Because I have found the most powerful love, self-love!

A lot of people have asked me: What was the motive to take me from survive to thrive over and over again. I didn't know the answer until recently, and it is because I refuse to give up on living the best life that I can!

Life can take everything away from me, but it can't take the determination of being the best of myself. I have what it takes to create my desired life. Because I finally *believe* in myself! Believing in myself is a *choice*. I am not the most gifted or talented person, but I chose to believe anything is possible. I study, practice, and work harder than others. I take on my challenges, and I dig deep within myself to conquer fears. I am no longer sitting in the passenger seat and letting life drag me around. I am the driver of my own life now!

In this third year, I am ready to pursue my dream life at full speed! I may get knocked down again, but I will always get up and raise up even higher. All the hardships I have been through have prepared an ordinary person like me for an extraordinary destiny!

Today is the day that I say good-bye to my sorrow and say hello to a wonderful new life again!

What I Say to Myself Matters

"Loving or hating the life you are living is solely all in your repeated self-talk."
- Edmond Mbiaka

February 8, 2019 (Day 744)

Our emotions are often triggered by what others say or do to us. But the hard truth is really that what I say to myself matters. It is all about the stories that I tell myself to create the reality of my life.

The second year after I moved to America from China, I started working as a Chinese tutor at our local public schools to help a few Chinese kids. Most of those students spoke almost no English. At that time, my English was quite limited as well. I felt very uncomfortable with speaking and writing during our weekly tutor meeting. I took notes by writing it in Chinese, other tutors laughed at me. I felt embarrassed when other tutors corrected me with certain pronunciations. I felt they thought I was stupid because I couldn't speak English.

I hated my job, but I didn't want to lose it since we were very tight on money at that moment. One day, one of my fourth-grade Chinese girls came to me with a big smile on her face. She told me that she thought she was very special because she's Chinese. What made her believe so is because there were so many people in her class that wanted to be her friend. In my head, I was like *Wow, I am Chinese too, but all I felt was that no one likes me!*

Now when I look back, I realized these opposite feelings were caused by what we said to ourselves. I told myself a victim story, and she told herself an adventure story. I could tell myself that other tutors were helping me with my pronunciations, instead of they were criticizing me or trying to embarrass me. I could tell myself that I was pretty awesome that I went to volunteer at the school and the principal loved me so much they offered me this job. I often forget how many great things that I have achieved (like getting this tutor job) and only focus on what I didn't do very well at that moment (like my English skills).

When I was little, my mom, and her side of family, often told me that I was such an ugly girl and that I looked just like my dad. Even my brother sometimes would say things like "No matter what beautiful clothes you put on; you just don't look good." As a young girl, I believed them. I believed that I am not a good-looking girl.

When I was thirty years old and met Bob in Shanghai, he was the first one who ever said to me "You are beautiful!" I was like, *I don't think so. What do you want from me?* Then I moved to America and there were more and more people telling me that I was beautiful. I didn't believe them and thought they were just being polite. Four years ago, when I started my blogging career, there were even more people telling me that I was beautiful on a daily basis. But I still didn't believe.

It wasn't until last year I finally believed that I was beautiful whole-heartedly. It took me forty-four years to believe that I am beautiful. Why? Because the beliefs that I had programmed and conditioned when I was young were so powerful. It ran for so many years and it ran automatically without me even knowing it. *I am ugly* was the self-talk story that I kept telling myself.

Last year I started to learn more about myself and realized those blocks are just some ill beliefs that I was conditioned with when I was little. Now as a grown-up and capable women, I have the ability to remove those nonsense beliefs and replace them with very positive and loving self-talks and stories.

Nowadays, here is what I say to myself when I look in the mirror "You are beautiful inside and out. You are capable to achieve your goals. You are good enough to deserve all the loves and joys in your life." What do you say to yourself?

Re-entering the Dating World in My Forties

"You either like me or you don't. It took me forty-something years to learn how to love myself. I don't have that kind of time to convince someone else."

- Unknown

February 14, 2019 (Day 750)

It has been more than two years since I lost my husband; my best friend and my soulmate. I often call myself the master of survivals. I have come to the conclusion that there are no situations that I can't get out of and turn into a happy ending. All the suffering that I had been through has turned me into this strong and happy woman who has laser focus on my dreams and determined to be the best I can be.

What I have learned is I don't need anyone to remind me how amazing I am. I acknowledge how much I have achieved. I don't need anyone to take care of me. I know how to take very good care of myself. I eat healthy and sleep well. I've got my high school body back. I don't need anyone to pay my bills or buy me luxury handbags, I am financially independent and don't mind spoiling myself once in a while. I don't feel lonely, although I live alone. I really enjoy learning, reading, creating, and helping others. The bottom line is I don't need anyone to complete me. I have completed myself!

I am really glad that I took the time to be with myself and learn about who I am before I re-entered the dating world. At this point of my life, I am not emotionally handicapped. I just want to find a kind soul who is loving life and striving to be the best of himself. I want someone to share this amazing life with. So, I am very careful and picky about who I want in my life.

For the first time, I came up with a list of twenty-seven things my soulmate looks like. Warm smile, nice gentleman and positive thinker made the top three. I told everyone that I was chatting with on the dating app that I will need at least three days of communication online to decide if I feel comfortable to exchange phone numbers and move to texting. There are still a few days before the phone calls happen. If the phone calls go well for a few days, then maybe there is the possibility to finally meet.

During this process, there were many men filtered out for many reasons. All the guys I have gone out with are all nice gentlemen who respected me and fit in with many of the items on my list. I told those gentlemen that I felt more comfortable to go out as friends first and see where it leads us. The first few dates were always just like meeting a new friend without all of the dating pressure. I usually told them after twenty-four hours if I felt the chemistry. It was hard at first to just tell them that I didn't feel it, but they all appreciated my honesty.

Whether you're seeking love for the first time or are starting again, over-forty-dating can feel daunting. But with all the self-love I have learned, I know I am worthy. The right man would respect my feelings, be willing to communicate, and to wait for a little bit longer before becoming romantic. I am very glad that I have completed myself before seeking my new love and hold a high standard about what I want. I have the confidence that I deserve the best love because I am enough! No mediocre love for me!

The Real Self-Love

"Love yourself instead of abusing yourself."
- Karolina Kurkova

March 22, 2019 (Day 784)

What is real self-love? Some people think self-love is self-care. For example, a lazy doing nothing day, a bubble bath, a massage and a Netflix day. Some people think self-love is when they do whatever to please themselves. For example, buying a designer's handbag, booking an exotic vacation, or becoming a serial dater just to have fun.

Self-love for me is not just those things we do to please ourselves on the surface. *Self-love is an on-going process of soul searching and becoming my best self.* Someone may ask, "What if you reach your 'ideal' self? But there will always be a new level to claim, a new goal to achieve. Does it mean that you will never be happy or satisfied with yourself?" Of course not, it just means you are finding happiness in your growth as a person. The real happiness for me is not the result, not the goal that I have achieved, it is the progress that I have made along the way. I celebrate every little step that I have taken and live in the present enjoying what growth I see daily.

Self-love also means having my best relationship with myself. That means I will not beat myself down when things are not going well. When I fail or start to doubt myself, I become my own cheerleader. I remind myself that I have a pure heart and always want to do well. I remind myself what a wonderful human being I am, and how many great things I have achieved in my life. I forgive myself if I have made mistakes and put effort to learn from them. I give myself permission to break down, to cry, and to not know what to do. I say *I LOVE YOU* every morning when I wake up and evening when I go to sleep along with giving all my gratitude to others that have helped along the way.

Self-love means to accept who I am as a human being who has endless potential. Some people don't really understand this one, they think self-love is just settling for what they have gotten. They accept giving up on their dreams because it is too hard to pursue, and they are not willing to put three years of their life on hold to make it happen. They accept being overweight and unhealthy because it is too hard to go to the gym regularly and eat a healthy daily. They try but give up too fast and don't stick with it long enough to see the results. They accept an okay relationship because it is too hard to confront their partner. They don't want to talk through their true feelings or find a solution with their partner when conflict appears. Does this sound familiar to you?

I have accepted that I am forty-five years old. That it is okay that my eyesight is changing and to have more and more grey hair. But it is not okay to not take care of my skin, my weight, and my appearance. I have accepted that I will always have an accent when I speak English. But it is not okay to use this as an excuse to not pursue my public speaking dream and write my books. I have accepted that I am a widow. That it is okay to be a little moody during the holidays. That it is okay to cry once in a while when something unexpectedly triggers a memory. But it is not okay to stay there and feel sorry for myself. I have accepted that I am a single woman again. That it is okay to not know how to date and struggle. But it is not okay to not learn.

Self-love is not just about buying myself followers. In fact, practicing self-love most of the times can be quite challenging and painful. Self-love is definitely tough love to me. Because I am breaking the old me in order for the new me to be born. It means I take 100% responsibility with my life as is today, the good, the bad and the ugly, they are all on me. It is hard to accept that I have contributed to what my life is. I didn't ask for the abuse as a child, and I can't say that it was my fault that my mom treated me that way. But I take 100% responsibility in healing myself and finding meaning in those life events. I am the one who has the duty to replace the pain with peace.

For me, *self-love also means self-discipline.* On evenings or weekends when everyone goes home to relax, I am still working to make it one step closer to my next goal. I don't watch TV, don't use social media much, and don't read any news. Instead, I listen to motivational speeches every morning. I read books and write reflections and a gratitude journal. My life is not just about working hard, I put a mask on daily to take care of my skin, I make sure to get at least eight hours of sleep, I get ninety-minute massages twice a month and I stay on a low-carb diet. I work for six weeks and then give myself a relaxing vacation to reward and celebrate.

Do you truly love yourself? Are you still beating yourself down when something goes wrong? Are you lonely when you are alone? Share your practice in defining and reaching your own level of self-love!

Breaking Through the Childhood Abuse and Neglect

*"From every wound there is a scar, and every scar tells a story.
Turn your wounds into wisdom."*
-Anonymous

April 5, 2019 (Day 798)

Some pain just doesn't heal over time. For me, the pain of my childhood abuse and neglect from my mom seems like a disease that no matter how hard I try to forget or to move on, it still comes back to haunt me over and over again. Every time when I think I am done with it; it has come back in a different form to show me its power. The emotional abuse still lingers there and affects my behaviors in so many unnoticeable ways.

I'm a forty-five-year-old woman who runs my own business, has my own family, but often feels hopeless to deal with this pain. It just doesn't go away! The symptoms are constantly worrying about doing something wrong, low self-esteem which makes me feel like I am not good enough to reach my big goals or deserve to live my wild dream life, becoming a workaholic to avoid insecurity, constantly feeling stressed, having a hard time to relax or feel safe, and struggling with close/intimate relationships where I feel like I have to be perfect so I will be loved.

Since I was damaged as a child, I have enough reasons to be sad and blame everything on my mom, right? Absolutely NOT! I am not that powerless little girl anymore. I know I need to find a way to heal and free myself. In the past few years, I have done a lot of work on myself. I have reached the level that I understand why she did what she did. I understand she treated me as she was treated when she was growing up. That was all she knew how to treat a daughter. I understand with very little food, clothes, and other resources, the culture favored the boys, so girls got whatever was left. She did what she thought was right to take care of the most important person, my older brother, so he could carry out our family name. But I disagree with her choice. So, I have been stuck here for about one year now.

A few weeks ago, after my regular gym class, I took the yoga class. I always see yoga as my treat to myself because I just love the mind, body, and spirit connections. I was lying on my yoga mat clearing out my mind after a long working day. The joy of being alive and doing what I love came to me. I said in my head, *thank you God for giving me this life so I can enjoy everything it has to offer.* I can feel my smile on my face even with my eyes closed. *I love you, God!* My inner dialogue continued.

Then a question suddenly came to my head. *If I can say, "I love you" to God, should I say the same thing to my actual parents? They were the ones who gave me this body and raised me up, right?* For my dad, we never had a very close relationship. He never stood up for me while my mom was treating me like I was trash, but he never really hurt me intentionally either. So, the answer is, YES! I love him. Although I have never said that to him, and he never said that to me either. Or maybe since he had passed away when I was in high school, it is easier to forgive someone who has long been gone. What about my mom? My thoughts were like, *THERE IS NO WAY! I HATE her and I will never say I LOVE YOU to her!* I felt my breath became fast and the anger started to rise. So, I told myself, I understand her, and I want to forgive her. But the anger just kept rising up. Suddenly, another question came to my head. *Would she die for me if my life was in danger at this moment?* My answer was *YES* without any hesitation. I was shocked and tears came to my eyes. So, my heart knows she LOVES me! My whole life I was longing for her love! But I forgot how she fought with strangers who had treated me badly in the public. I had forgotten she was the one who stayed with me and held me tight when the horse carriage crashed (when I was very little). My dad jumped off the carriage, but she chose to stay!

My tears were running down my face while I was laying on my yoga mat. My heart was so happy, and I knew I had finally found the answer and set myself free. She had said she was sorry and told me she cared about me. At the time I didn't believe her, but now I did! She wasn't the typical loving mom figure and she probably never will be. But she loves me, and that is all I needed to know! When I got home, I called her, and she was so surprised and happy to chat with me. I didn't tell her that I love her. That may scare her, and she would worry that something was wrong! But in my heart, I have said it many times to her. I am still struggling with the idea of telling her verbally, but I have planned to do it on Mother's Day this year! She will cry!

The Healing Journey

to Self-Love

"I finally fully activated the love generator inside of me. I will no longer wait on someone like my mom to love me, I love myself and that's my lifelong responsibility."

\- Grace Liang

May 17, 2019 (Day 840)

Two weeks ago, during a meditation program called "Tree of Life in Train the Trainer with Jack Canfield," I had another breakthrough and felt the major healing from my abusive childhood.

My parents had an arranged marriage. They hated each other but still chose to stick together after daily fights. We were super poor with a dirt floor, straw roof and no running water, indoor toilet or electricity. I had been claimed as worthless by my mom. According to her, no one would love me since I was so ugly and have a very bad personality. According to her, I was lazy, badly behaved and useless. She told me to shut-up when I sang because my voice was so painful to her ears. She laughed at my goals and said that the only thing I was good at was daydreaming. She yelled at me for embarrassing her because my boobs were too big.

When I was about seven years old, I started to realize that my mom would not love me that much no matter how hard I tried.

It was lunch time on a summer day. My mom sent me out to play. I was very happy because she usually made me work around the house. I stopped at a couple friend's houses, but no one could hang out at that moment. So, I returned home. Before entering the front door, I felt like needed to use the outhouse behind our little mud house. When I walked by the back window, I saw something that suddenly broke my heart. My mom was handing over a hard-boiled egg to my older brother. When she noticed me standing there, she was trying to hide that egg. I suddenly understood why she let me go play. She only had one egg and she wanted to give it to my older brother.

Things like that had happened many times. My mom believed boys were more important than girls and my older brother was loved much more than I was.

I realized I was broken because I was raised by someone who was broken. She hurt me because of her pain. I also realized it wasn't my fault that I didn't get her love. She had issues and just used me to deal; instead of actually dealing with her own issues. I pity her because she has never really experienced true love and her whole life has been a struggle. I had a hard time truly forgiving her. There have been many women in similar situations, and they didn't turn around to hurt their daughters. That's purely her choice.

During training with Jack Canfield two weeks ago, I realized that I had a limited belief. I didn't think I was good enough to conquer some giant goals. I still had resentment towards my mom.

On the fifth day of training, we did a new meditation and Jack took us to many places I have never thought I could go. I saw Mother Earth in my mind, and she showed me the unconditional love that a mother gives to her beloved child. Before I left, she told me to come visit any time when I need her. That was the moment I finally freed myself and forgave my mom. I came to a conclusion that the mother figure I have been longing for my whole life, the longing of true safety, security and being loved has always been inside of my heart. A great mom is the real human figure of the Mother Earth who came to your life to activate the love within you. Without this human figure, the unconditional love is still inside of me and I finally found the way to activate it completely by myself! I am not homeless anymore!! This unconditional love has been there since I was born, and it will be with me forever. When I need it, I just go back to it. It's my own self-love!

This is how I take 100% responsibility for my life to heal myself, to love myself unconditionally! I have finally fully activated the love generator inside of me. I will no longer wait on someone like my mom to love me, I love myself and that's my lifelong responsibility. I will not be disappointed or hurt by others, because I don't need them to make me feel loved and worthy, I *am* loved and worthy without a doubt! This love generator within me, not just supplies the self-love for me, but it also helps me give love to more people and a greater cause.

I have never known that I have this powerful source of love within me. Are you ready to heal yourself too?

ACKNOWLEDGMENTS

I want to dedicate this book to my late husband, Robert Buck. Before he passed away, he left me with a last piece of advice: "Don't rush! Follow your dream! Believe you are worth it!" He was the one who never judged me, and he was also the one who taught me to just simply enjoy life. My man was a good teacher, considering he taught me English. He also taught me to drive, party, travel, garden, and relax. Through our marriage, I experienced what unconditional love was. I know he feels very proud of his student, and now is showing off with all his new friends in heaven. "Look - that is my wife!"

There was no way I could have gotten through my grief journey without all of the support from my family and friends, especially my stepdaughter, Ashley Buck, and her fiancé Adam Cook. Both of my late husband's sisters often called me from California to check on me. I am very blessed that I still have a big and loving family after my man passed away.

I also would like to say thank you to those who have given me so much love and support during the darkest time of my life—my ex-co-workers at University Liggett School and the sweet students. Also, thank you to my super nice and helpful neighbors, my beloved blogging community, and my photographers.

Last but not least, thanks to my kindhearted readers and followers, those who sent me emails or messages or left very supportive comments. We may never get a chance to see each other, but I know at that moment we connected! In fact, this book became a reality all because of those readers. They have encouraged me to write this book for a long time.

About the Author

Grace Liang is a full-time Influencer based in Troy, Michigan. She is also a public speaker, and an Inner Power coach. She transforms people to get what they want, by using their body wisdom to activate their inner power and remove emotional blocks. Grace offers "Activate Your Inner Power" workshops, and online guided course. You can find out more at www.colorandgrace.com.

When she is not working, you can find her in her garden, or cooking up a storm to entertain her family and friends. She is also a big supporter of many charities. Recently, she has been fully funded to participate in the Susan G. Koman 3-Day Walk in Michigan to help fight against breast cancer.

Email: gracel@colorandgrace.com
Website: www.colorandgrace.com
Instagram: @colorandgrace
Facebook: @colorandgrace